SIMULATIONS

A Handbook for Teachers and Trainers

THIRD EDITION

KEN JONES

Kogan Page Ltd, London
Nichols Publishing Company,
New Jersey

First published in 1980
Second edition published in 1987
This third edition published in 1995

Kogan Page Limited
120 Pentonville Road
London N1 9JN

© Kenneth Jones, 1980, 1987, 1995

British Library Cataloguing in Publication Data

A CIP record for this book is available from the British Library.

ISBN 0 7494 1666 1

This third edition first published in the United States of America in 1995 by Nichols Publishing Company, PO Box 6036, East Brunswick, NJ 08816.

ISBN (USA) 0-89397-441-2

Contents

Preface

The dictionary definition of a simulation is misleading as it suggests that in a simulation the participants simulate (mimic, play act) and that the event is not real but pretence. The simulations in this book are not animated computer graphics, or maps, or representations – they are interactive events. In this sense it is the environment that is simulated – the company, the newsroom, the market place – but the behaviour is real. The power of a simulation arises from the reality of the communication skills, the analysis, the decision-making. The participants have functional or professional roles. They do not play act or mimic; if they did it would be role play or drama. They keep their own personalities but take on different jobs, duties and responsibilities. Unlike games, where everyone has the role of player with a duty to try to win, simulations require 'professional' behaviour, including professional ethics. A well-designed simulation provides enough key facts to allow the participants to function professionally.

This third edition is a substantial rewrite of the first two editions.

1. It keeps the same structure but has more up-to-date examples to help the facilitator choose, use, run and assess simulations.
2. It examines recent criticisms that some simulations, including the well-known STARPOWER, are unethical and psychologically harmful. My view is that although the particular criticism of STARPOWER is flawed, facilitators tend to have a blind spot in relation to methodology and ethics.

3. It develops a concept, 'real life', rarely mentioned in other books on interactive events, not merely as background information but as part of the action itself.
4. What the earlier editions referred to as 'mish-mash' events I now term 'ambivalents'. The book explains how to recognize, alter, or avoid them.
5. A survey of the British educational scene is omitted and replaced with a section dealing with social and cultural simulations.
6. The section on icebreakers has been extended and a complete icebreaker is given in the Appendix that can be photocopied for classroom use.
7. The name of the person running the events has changed. In the first edition it was *controller*, in the second it was *organizer* and in this edition it is *facilitator*. This is in line with current practice, to indicate the need for a hands-off approach during the action itself.

What has not changed is the advice to look at what actually happens in an event and not be misled by labels and definitions, or by aims or expectations. What does happen is more important than what 'should' happen.

The simulation technique is one of the most interesting and powerful of the techniques used in education and training. This new edition concentrates on ways of using simulations effectively and enjoyably.

Chapter 1

What's a simulation?

ESSENTIAL CHARACTERISTICS

In this book 'simulation' refers to a classroom event which has two essential characteristics:

1. The participants have functional roles – survivor, journalist, judge, fashion designer, Prime Minister.
2. Sufficient information is provided on an issue or a problem – memos, maps, newspaper items, documents, materials – to enable the participants to function as professionals.

In the action part of a simulation there is no teacher or trainer. The participants must have autonomy, including the power and the authority to make mistakes. The survivors must be allowed the opportunity to die, the journalists must be allowed the opportunity to miss the deadline, the cabinet ministers must be given the freedom to fail to discuss the main item on the agenda. Thus, a simulation must be a non-taught event. If it is taught then it is not a simulation.

Teachers who are not used to simulations often have difficulty at first in resisting the temptation to interfere in the action in an effort to help the participants 'succeed'. Habits of help, guidance and instruction are not easily placed in cold storage. There is no policeman to stop a teacher walking into the cabinet office and sitting down next to the Prime Minister and saying 'How are you getting on? Do you understand what you have to do? Have you consulted with your colleagues yet?'

A basic reason for using simulations is that mistakes are both inevitable and desirable. It is experiential learning, not programmed learning, or a rehearsed event. Participants learn from their mistakes and want the opportunity to improve in the next simulation. The greater the disaster, the greater the learning. Any anxieties felt by the facilitator that the participants 'may not get it right' are caused by a misunderstanding of the educational justification for simulations.

The provision of the key facts is essential. Simulations are not improvised drama, or episodic role play. They are not isolated events played out before an audience of fellow pupils/students. In a professional situation the participants must have the key facts, and not be asked to invent them. To say 'You are the customer returning a broken shoe, and you are the shop assistant' is not enough. Even though such role play may be functional rather than play acting, this is not sufficient in itself to make it a simulation. Role play usually involves a high degree of participant authorship. In the above example the participants would probably invent key facts. The customer might take on the role of author and invent the circumstances in which the shoe broke, where, when, and what were the consequences. The shop assistant could take on the role of author in order to invent the policy of the shop towards disgruntled customers who return articles. There is nothing wrong with this; imagination and improvisation are fine. But the thoughts, motives, and tasks of a participant in such a role play are quite different from a simulation. This is not to say that participants in simulations never invent 'facts', but they should never be the key facts, otherwise it is either a badly designed simulation or, if there is a significant degree of participant authorship, not a simulation at all.

NON-ESSENTIAL CHARACTERISTICS

A simulation does not have to attempt to reproduce reality. In fact, the more an author tries to reproduce the real world with all its complexities and irrelevancies, the more unworkable the event becomes.

It is not just that reality is often unworkable in the classroom, reality is not always desirable from an educational point of view. Some simulations deliberately distort reality, or turn it on its head in order to provide a contrast to reality, or an optional reality. There are simulations set in imaginary countries, or in pre-history, or in the future, or in a fantasy world. These are not non-simulations or sub-standard simulations. Factors which help produce a good simulation include plausibility and consistency, not attempts to duplicate the real world.

As readers of academic literature on simulations will realize, this rejection of 'representing reality' utterly contradicts the academic definition. According to SAGSET (Society for Interactive Learning) and ISAGA (International Simulation and Gaming Association) a simulation is

> A working representation of reality; it may be abstracted, simplified or accelerated model of the process. It allows students to explore systems where reality is too expensive, complex, dangerous, fast or slow.

This definition may be suitable for systems analysis, computer programs, model making and the like, but it does not reflect, in terminology or in content, the interactive human simulations referred to in this book. The terminology – 'representation', 'systems', 'models', 'students' – suggests no professional roles in non-taught events but a sort of programmed instruction geared to the fact-learning of things called models and systems. The jargon is indicative of the American approach to education, which tends to be based on step-by-step learning aimed at results which can be quantified by means of objective (and frequent) testing.

Another non-essential aspect of simulations is the view that simulations must have factual answers. Some do, some don't. A simulation is not the same as a puzzle, problem or textbook. Many of the most interesting simulations are open ended, and deal with values and opinions, emotions and attitudes. In such simulations the participants might well consider 'What questions should we ask?' rather than 'What answers should we give?'

It is not essential that a simulation should have clearly defined educational objectives. Aims and objectives are like hopes and expectations: they are not events and are not part of events. Naturally, authors and facilitators of events aim to achieve certain results but these are not necessarily part of the event itself. Indeed, some of the most famous and effective simulations are educationally ambiguous and the process is usually far more important than the end product. Because simulations are 'owned' by the participants it is advisable to formulate aims on the basis of what actually happens rather than on what is supposed to happen.

Nor is it essential that the action part of a good simulation should include effective learning. Experiential learning frequently occurs after rather than during an event. The action part of a simulation can include muddle and mistakes, and participants can become completely convinced that their own arguments and solutions are the best, and that other people are being unreasonable. Very often participants will believe that if something goes wrong it must be someone else's fault rather than their own. This does not make the event a non-simulation or a bad simulation. In a simulation it is not a crime to make mistakes, the crime is not to learn from the experience.

One advantage of simulations is that they have debriefings, a period after the event for an appraisal of what really happened. Learning from experience must allow time for reflection on that experience, and the opportunity to try again. Instant enlightenment is no more an essential feature of simulations than it is of life outside the classroom.

BOUNDARY LINES

Simulations are non-taught events. They are best characterized not by their titles or by their aims, but by what actually goes on in the minds of the participants. Therefore, the thoughts and attitudes, and the emotions and behaviour, are the evidence for distinguishing between simulations and other interactive techniques.

Boundary lines cannot be drawn between techniques merely by inspecting the documents. For example, the document in a case study could be identical to those in a simulation. The difference is that in a case study the students are looking at an event from the outside for the purpose of gaining knowledge, whereas in a simulation they are on the inside, with the power and authority of professionals who are trying to cope with a developing situation. This is an extremely important difference.

It is not enough to inspect the format. To an observer who walks into a classroom and witnesses a few minutes of a discussion between participants in the role of government ministers there might be little if any indication whether the event was role play or a simulation. Boundary drawing requires evidence of motives and thoughts. If the participants were:

(a)   imitating particular people or stereotypes, and/or
(b)   inventing key facts about the subject matter, and/or
(c)   thinking of themselves as students taking a role under the supervision of the teacher

then the activity would be in the field of drama in the case of (a), authorship in (b), and tuition in (c). But if, before the observer arrived, the participants had spent some time delving into the 'facts' about the issue, and were thinking professionally, then it would be a simulation.

Games share with simulations the essential criteria of autonomy. Once the action begins neither of them can be taught without changing the technique into something different – into a coaching session, a guided exercise, etc. The players in a game and the participants in a simulation are in charge within their particular environment, but only so long as they accept the conditions. The players in a game must accept the rules and must accept full professional responsibilities. If these conditions are not met, then the activity requires another label.

Suppose, for example, that after a game of Monopoly one of the 'players' says, 'I did not try to win because I did not think it was right to knock down houses in order to build hotels'. This reveals that the person was not a player as defined or implied in the rules of the game, and for that person the event was not a game.

Games do not have real-world ethics whereas simulations usually include real-world ethics. This is a key distinction when drawing boundary lines. Suppose an event is labelled OUR TOWN DEVELOPMENT GAME and the only roles are property developers, the winner being the group to make the most profit. Afterwards, one group says 'We won because we gained the most profit by building a nuclear plant next to the railway station' then they deserve praise, not blame; they had behaved responsibly by fulfilling their duty to try to win. The event was a game, not a simulation. But if the roles for the property developers had said something like 'Company reputations matter as well as profits' and did not refer to 'winners', then clearly the event was intended to be a simulation since real-world reputations involve real-world ethics. In this event any proposal to develop a nuclear plant in a town would be discussed in relation to ethics, particularly environmental questions.

TERMINOLOGY

It follows from the demarcation of territories that a simulation can go terribly wrong if the organizer uses inappropriate terminology. The wrong words lead to the wrong expectations, and the wrong expectations lead to the wrong behaviour.

Since the language of gaming and the theatre slip easily off the tongue it can be useful to draw up a list of words and phrases which could be used to introduce simulations and, more importantly, a list of words and phrases which could sabotage the event.

The lists below of 'appropriate' and 'inappropriate' words and phrases could serve as a starting point. There is a loose but not exact correspondence between pairs of items in each list.

Appropriate	*Inappropriate*
simulation, activity, event	game drama, role play, exercise
participant	player, actor, puzzler, trainee, student
facilitator (or organizer)	teacher, trainer, instructor
behaviour, function, profession	playing, acting, staging puzzling
role (functional)	role (acting a part)
real-world responsible behaviour	winning (losing) the game
real-world ethics	point scoring, having fun
professional conduct	performing the exercise (game, etc)

Naturally, the meaning of the above words depends on the context. Thus, in a simulation about a court case or a legislature it would be appropriate to say 'We won (lost)' but this would be shorthand for saying 'We won (lost) the case', or 'We won (lost) the vote', but not 'We won (lost) the game'.

The 'inappropriate' list is not intended to reflect adversely on the techniques of games, informal drama and exercises. Games can be serious as well as fun, and drama can involve far more than just acting. The intention is simply to underline the fact that words carry with them all sorts of associated baggage and, until simulations become a familiar experience, both facilitators and participants are easy victims of inadvertent sabotage by using the wrong labels. As will be argued in later chapters, a clear appreciation of boundary lines helps immeasurably in choosing suitable simulations, designing and running the events, evaluating the materials and assessing the behaviour, including both oral and written skills.

One other usage of the word simulation is worth noting. Like the words 'drama', 'exercise' and 'game' the word 'simulation' is often used as shorthand to mean the materials on which the event is based. In this sense one can say, 'We have plenty of plays (exercises, games, simulations) in the library'. There is usually no difficulty in discriminating between the two meanings within the context. Although the two meanings – event and materials – usually go arm in arm, this book does concentrate on simulations as events, and it is useful to try to get into the habit of visualizing simulations in terms of people rather than paper.

MODES OF THOUGHT AND BEHAVIOUR

Modes of thought and behaviour can usefully distinguish the different interactive methodologies:

Real life

This category is hardly mentioned in the literature on interactive events, but it is worth discussing in relation to appropriate and consistent behaviour. Most academics take 'real life' to mean 'That which is outside a game (simulation, role play, or exercise)'. This is misleading. There are four different types of 'real life' which may occur: reference points, consequences, mimicry and intrusions.

Reference points

As reference points 'real life' refers to that which is normal, customary, legal, and so on. It establishes within a simulation a common code of behaviour and a set of procedures. For example, in a committee-meeting simulation, someone might point out that it is usual to vote on the amendment before voting on the motion itself. In this sense real life sets boundaries and guidelines. But 'real life' is not the same as the 'real world'. The author of a simulation need not try to copy the real world. A simulation on the flightdeck of an inter-galactic space ship can also have a committee which votes on the amendment before voting on the motion; that too would be a 'real life' reference point.

Consequences

Real life is usually long-term. To 'win' or to 'lose' has consequences beyond marking up a score. In particular, real life has ethics, reputations, retribution, and revenge. Whereas selfishness is quite legitimate in a game, role play or exercise, it can seriously damage reputations in real life and in simulations. Probably the most vulnerable are those people who play a simulation as though it were a game. In the debriefing of a simulation, it is quite proper for the facilitator to ask: 'You secured this contract by lying and cheating, but what do you think the long-term consequences would be?'

Mimicry

Mimicry of 'real life' is legitimate for actors in role play and drama but not for participants in a simulation. In the debriefing all participants should be able to give reasons for their behaviour and not say 'I was just imitating that person I saw on television last night.' I once ran a course on simulations for drama and primary school teachers. I explained the difference between simulations and role play/drama. The teachers, divided into groups, devised their own simulations and ran these, with their colleagues from other groups being the participants. One simulation postulated a society of the future where tests were used to divide citizens into 'workers' and 'drones'. One of those to be tested led a successful revolt and no one entered the assessment room until I appealed for fairness to allow their colleagues' simulation to work. Later I asked the dissident in private whether he had considered that his revolt might have damaged his prospects in the hypothetical society. 'Oh yes, I knew it would probably do me no good at all, but I have just been made head of drama at my school and I wanted to create as much drama as possible.'

Intrusions

'Real life' as an intrusion takes many forms and is far more prevalent than commonly supposed. It can be helpful or disruptive and the effects vary according to the methodology. In an interactive event the facilitator might ask 'Do you want to break now or later?' At this point the participants, players, problem solvers and actors have to step out of their behaviour mode into the real world. Since facilitators usually recognize that interactive events bestow a great deal of participant autonomy (they 'own' the event) it follows that most real-world interruptions come from the participants. If a bridge player says 'You are cheating' the utterance is not made in a player mode but in a real-life mode. Suppose that during the running of a business simulation for trainers a participant says 'This simulation will be excellent for my new intake of trainees'. At this point the person has abandoned the business role and is, unwittingly or otherwise, sabotaging the event by inviting the others to step over the borderline into the real world.

A more fundamental type of intrusion of real life is to introduce real money into a simulation as a reward for 'winning'. Sometimes this is an author-created intrusion, sometimes facilitator-created. It is almost always bad. For a participant to lose real money during a simulation, even only a small coin, can create a trauma far in excess of the amount lost. Even if the participants agree at the beginning to put in a sum of money, and even if the facilitator offers to return the sum lost to the aggrieved person, the hurt and unpleasantness can remain. Participants usually feel they have been set up and the facilitator gets the blame. (See THE COMMONS GAME (page 27 for an example of real-money intrusion and STARPOWER (page 29 for real-lollipop intrusion).

Simulations

For the purpose of this book, a simulation is an event in which the participants have (functional) roles, duties and sufficient key information about the problems to carry out these duties without play acting or inventing key facts. They keep their own person- alities but take on a job, duties, responsibilities and do the best they can in the situation in which they find themselves.

Role plays

As with simulations, role plays have roles but the emphasis is usually on 'play' – that is, acting a part, mimicking, and imitating. Those role plays which are functional ('You are a diner ordering a meal') are usually brief, are often performed with an audience and usually have a minimum of background information. Conse- quently, participants have the role of authors – they invent much of their scenario. This is a point often overlooked by observers.

Games

Whatever the motive for running a game (enjoyment, education, or competition) all the participants are in one role – players. (A referee is not a participant in the game.) As players, they have a duty to try to win and a scoring mechanism is provided to enable them to ascertain winners and losers.

Exercises

In classroom-type exercises the role is usually that of problem solver, puzzler, or decision-maker. The participants remain themselves. In thinking about the problems and discussing what to do, they see the problems from the outside whereas with simulations and role plays the problems are seen from the inside. The thoughts are dispassionate: 'They might be killed if they went north', not 'We might be killed if we went north'. Since the participants remain themselves in the real world it is easier for them to have access to the facilitator than in simulations, role plays or games when they would have to step out of role to ask for information or advice. 'Are we allowed to use rulers?' is a compatible question to a facilitator in an exercise. (In a simulation the facilitator might reply 'You are the architects and planners, not me'.) Exercises can become games if the event is competitive, has a scoring mechanism and if the participants (players) have a duty to try to win irrespective of real-world ethics. Exercises can become simulations if the participants are given roles and sufficient information to tackle the problems.

Ambivalents

An ambivalent is my term for an interactive event in which incompatible and conflicting methodologies operate simultaneously. They do not fit into any other class, by definition. Experience suggests that there are a great many such events and that they can do considerable harm on a personal and interpersonal level. The symptoms of an ambivalent are that the facilitator and participants do not understand what has gone wrong. The facilitator blames the participants (usually alleging greed and selfishness) and the participants blame each other. Both sides fail to realize that there has been a clash of incompatible methodologies. They tend to interpret it as a clash of personalities or evidence of reprehensible behaviour. Characteristics of reporting events are: (a) such muddled terminology with labels used interchangeably; (b) an unawareness that incompatibility occurred within the specific event; and (c) a general unawareness that a clash of incompatible methodologies was even a possibility.

> After many DENTIST sessions we conclude that the actors only look for a joint effort once it has become clear that there is no single clear winner. At the end of a simulation we have observed that occasionally actors try to tilt the game to collect a huge profit or maybe to satisfy their greed. (Klabbers and Hearn 1988)

One of the most significant aspects of this study, however, did not show up in the data analysis. It is the extreme seriousness with which the subjects take the problems. Comments such as 'If you defect on the rest of us, you're going to live with it for the rest of your life' were not uncommon. Nor was it unusual for people to wish to leave the experimental building by the back door, to claim that they did not wish to see the 'sons of bitches' who double-crossed them, to become extremely angry at other subjects, or to become tearful. (Liebrand 1983)

The second account refers to PRISONER'S DILEMMA. Two people are jointly charged with a crime and have to plead separately and without consultation. The worst outcome is to plead not guilty when one's companion pleads guilty. If this event is run in serial form, repeating the decision-making after learning how the co-defendant pleaded in the previous round, it is almost inevitably an ambivalent. If all the participants thought it was a game they would always avoid losing by pleading guilty. If all thought it was a simulation they would all plead not guilty out of loyalty to their companion. Undoubtedly the 'sons of bitches' were the gamesters who played to win and their accusers were those in the simulation mode who had the duties and obligations of fellow prisoners. Liebrand himself refers to PRISONER'S DILEMMA as a 'social dilemma game' – and presumably described it as such in the briefing. Not to have realized the explosive potential (and to have omitted a debriefing) was like being in charge of a runaway train without a driver's manual.

Although this last example is extreme, it serves to highlight the dangers, not only to relations between participants but the relationships between facilitator and participants. The missing element in such accounts is what the participants said afterwards about the facilitator. Another element which tends to go unreported is what was said at the debriefing. For example, were the participants in DENTIST criticized openly, or did the facilitators privately form an impression of the characters and personalities of those accused of being greedy or uncaring?

Unfortunately, much of the academic literature on interactive events is not only lacking in practical descriptions of what happened, it is utterly confusing on terminology. Many authors use one specific term as an umbrella word – usually calling all interactive events 'games' or 'exercises'. The authors then have difficulty in referring to the original meaning of the promoted word. They seem to be saying 'This simulation is a game, this exercise is a game, this role play is a game and this game is a game.'

Other academics try to solve the boundary problem by recourse to hyphenated terms – simulation-games and so on. This would be acceptable if they meant 'simulations and games' or 'simulations or games' – two separate identities under the same label. But simulation-game is usually postulated as a third and separate methodology. A much-quoted definition is:

A simulation-game combines the features of a game (competition, co-operation, rules, players) with those of a simulation (incorporation of features of the real world).

This is what I call an ambivalent. It is like saying 'Oil–water is a mixture of oil and water'. The fact is, games have players with the duty of trying to win and this behaviour is psychologically incompatible with the functional (professional, ethical, real-world) behaviour of participants in a simulation.

In any case, the above definition of a simulation-game is confused and contradictory. While most people would accept that competition is a feature of a game, few people would say that cooperation was a necessary element in a game – apart from co-operation within a team. Nor is there any clear distinction between 'features of the real world' on the one hand and 'competition, co-operation rule, players' on the other. After all, real-world features include competition, cooperation and rules. The only merit of the definition is that it associates games with the term 'players' – games require player-behaviour otherwise the event is not a game, it is something else.

It is clear from reading accounts of interactive events that an appreciation of methodology is a much neglected essential. Unfortunately, facilitators tend to assume that the events they run are consistent – which is not surprising if the facilitators lack the concepts which can reveal inconsistencies. Even the denials of inconsistency sometimes contain evidence of muddle. The following example is only a slight exaggeration:

Some facilitators may run muddled games but when I run an exercise my students take the role of actors and behave consistently as players in the simulation.

It is not only the design of the simulation or the way it is introduced which can cause differing expectations and conflicting modes of behaviour among the participants. If the setting is a drama class the expectations are likely to be of drama and if the facilitator does not make it clear that play acting is forbidden, there is a serious danger of some participants treating the simulation professionally while others behave in a drama mode.

The argument here is not semantic. The issue is not definitions. What matters is what actually happens during the event. Is the behaviour consistent? For example, if everyone called an event a game but everyone behaved as if it were a simulation then the event would be a simulation. It would not be a game or an ambivalent. Similarly, if everyone called the event a simulation but behaved in the gaming mode it would be a game, not a simulation or an ambivalent. Consistency of behaviour is the issue. The argument is not about definitions, it is about real people and real people can get hurt.

HOW TO AVOID AMBIVALENTS

As pointed out in the last section, ambivalents are dangerous. They can hurt. They can damage feelings, friendships, and reputations. The very fact that an ambivalent occurs means that those involved, particularly the facilitator, are usually unaware of the situation. Unfortunately, it is not uncommon for facilitators to congratulate themselves that an event went well apart from one or two participants who were greedy, irresponsible, feckless, and so on. Ambivalents can be thought of as falling into three broad categories: those created by (a) the author of the event; (b) the facilitator; and (c) the participants. The value of this categorization is that muddles can be treated at source. If the author is at fault the event can be altered so as to make it consistent. If the facilitator introduces inconsistency then the answer is for the facilitator to hone the skills of differentiating between methodologies. If a few of the participants abdicate their duties and behave in an inconsistent mode then this, too, can be dealt with at source.

Author-created ambivalents

Some authors, especially Americans, often build into the event inappropriate point-scoring mechanisms either for gaming reasons or for the purpose of educational assessment. In a simulation about an assembly it is appropriate to count votes, but it is not appropriate to award a hundred marks for people who introduce successful resolutions, fifty marks for successful amendments, and ten marks for every minute a person speaks. Are the participants supposed to behave as parliamentarians or as gamesters? I was once asked by a publisher if I would incorporate into a parliamentary simulation a form with two columns headed 'Points we agree on', 'Points we disagree on', which would be given to each Member of Parliament to carry around and fill in. As well as being implausible, it would have introduced an irreconcilable conflict between the thoughts of and behaviour of students and the thoughts and behaviour of parliamentarians.

Similar conflicts occur in simulation-dramas between professional conduct and acting. The instructions in a simulation-drama about business could say 'Participants must try to behave in the best interests of their company' and the role cards say 'You are a friendly supervisor', 'You are a disgruntled sales representative'. Depending on circumstances, it could be in the best interests of the company for the supervisor to be non-friendly or the sales representative to be non-disgruntled. It is not unusual for a political simulation to have a role card saying something on the lines of 'You are a rebel leader and you are angry because . . .' This requires the acting of anger, and suggests to the participant that the behaviour should be not only highly emotional but also stupid. It deprives the participant of the opportunity of behaving in other ways which may be more suitable in the circumstances. It need take only one participant to start ham acting for others to follow suit and a situation can arise where half the group are trying to take it seriously while the other half are mimicking and play acting.

Alert facilitators can usually rescue an author-created ambivalent. Contradictions can be removed, role cards altered, rules rewritten and the methodology clearly explained. Indeed, if the participants themselves know the differences between (a) gaming, (b) acting and (c) professional conduct, they can ignore the contradictions and all treat the event as a game, as role play or as a simulation. Consistent events, by definition, cannot be ambivalents.

Facilitator-created ambivalents

Facilitators can create ambivalents in many ways – inappropriate terminology, introducing incompatible features from the real world, interfering with participant decision-making to try to ensure 'success', etc. Facilitators can also create ambivalents by inaction. For example, if the facilitator tries to run a simulation in a drama class without explaining that professional type behaviour is required and that play acting is inappropriate, then an ambivalent is likely to occur, with some participants trying to comply with functional duties of their role, while others are putting on a performance and staging a drama. If, of course, everyone treats it as a play acting session then that is what it will be – not an ambivalent. Similarly, if the context is one where the participants are used to competitive games and have never participated in a simulation and the facilitator fails to explain the methodology, the result is likely to be an ambivalent.

Participant-created ambivalents

Ambivalents created by one or two participants are quite common, particularly if the participants have not been briefed about what a simulation is and what it is not. The best way to deal with this is to note the change in the category of behaviour of the disrupter. A participant may move into:

(a) the real-world category: 'I might use this simulation at my youth club';
(b) the role play category which can include authorship: 'My country has lots of nuclear weapons and we have just bombed your country, so you are dead'; or
(c) the gaming category: 'We don't care about all those unem-

ployed people, we have the most tokens and so we have won the game'.

Unlike games and exercises, simulations allow facilitators to take an appropriate role to get an event back on course. In a business simulation the facilitator can take on the role of an usher or secretary to tell the disrupter that there is an important telephone call. Having extracted the person from the event the facilitator can then discuss the situation. Usually the cause of the trouble is a misunderstanding – the participant was unclear of the distinction between methodologies. However, if it is serious the person can retire from the event or continue in a different role.

ANATOMY OF AN AMBIVALENT

It might be thought from the previous section that all ambivalents are bad and should be avoided. This is true except for very rare cases of 'necessary' ambivalents. These are necessary because they would not work properly if every participant was in the same methodology. A few of the most powerful and well-known interactive events are necessary ambivalents and because they are so widely known it is useful to analyse the potential clash of methodologies. The best known example is STARPOWER by Garry Shirts, recently the subject of some severe criticisms. But before considering this event, it is useful to look at a simpler, yet revealing, ambivalent, THE COMMONS GAME by Richard Powers, in order to clarify some of the issues.

THE COMMONS GAME is a relatively straightforward example of a necessary ambivalent. The format does not change and the same procedures remain in force throughout the event. The participants sit in a group and shields are provided so that each person can play a coloured card privately. The facilitator walks around the group and notes which cards have been played and announces the total; for example, 'Four red cards and one orange card'. The facilitator does not reveal who played which card but gives the score for the whole group for that round. Individuals keep their own scores and between rounds they can discuss and agree/disagree on what cards to play. Whether they play the card they agreed to play is another matter.

Treated as a game

The event is labelled 'game' and the use of abstract cards suggests it is a game. If everyone treats it as a game, players will try to maximize their own scores irrespective of the group's score. The aim will be to score more points than any of the other players and the consequent low group score is irrelevant since the winner in a low-scoring game is just as much a winner as in a high-scoring game. Thus, everyone would always play the green card which gains the maximum personal points. To play anything other than a green card would risk losing. There would be nothing to say in the discussion periods since everyone would be in the gaming mode and trying to win and they would all know this. To play any card other than a green card would be to score less and thus contrary to the duty of a player. After a few rounds the repetition of green-card play would become completely predictable and therefore utterly boring.

Treated as a simulation

If everyone treated the event as a simulation, each participant would be free of any gaming duty. Instead of starting to play cards in the gaming mode the group would probably discuss the situation in the simulation mode in their roles as users of the common land. Their concern would be to maximize group wealth, which would also maximize individual wealth. The problem is simply solved. Everyone plays the red card except for one participant who plays the lower-scoring orange card which enhances the total score of the whole group. The participants could take it in turns to play the orange card. To avoid devious and greedy behaviour (someone playing the green card) the group could lay aside the shields. A consistent simulation mode, as with the consistent gaming mode, is likely to produce a predictable and boring event.

Treated as an ambivalent

Almost inevitably the event is an ambivalent. Naturally, the participants do not treat it as an ambivalent, they make it one unwittingly. Some start in the gaming mode, some in the simulation mode, and some change modes during the course of the event. Some participants are likely to be in a state of confusion. They are unaware of the ethics of the event. Is it ethical to try to 'win', as in a game, or is it unethical as in a simulation about co-operating for the common good? The participants are unlikely to sort out the muddle and will probably be unaware that there is a muddle. As usual, the potential victims are likely to be the gamesters. The subsequent accusations from the simulation-mode participants (reinforced by the facilitator) could be on the lines of 'Why were you so greedy? You won, so you must have played the green card when you told us you were playing the red card. You lied and did not care about the community at all. You were just out for yourself all the time.' The gamesters might reply 'It was just a game, wasn't it? We were supposed to be having fun. Why are you so serious, haven't you got a sense of humour? Anyway, we won.'

For THE COMMONS GAME to work there has to be a subtle form of deceit practised by the facilitator. In briefing the event the facilitator cannot say 'This is a game and you all have a duty to try to win', nor 'You are in the role of leaders of your community and have a duty to increase its wealth'. If asked 'What is the object of this event?' the facilitator's best bet is to preserve the deceit with a non-committal reply. However, most facilitators know nothing about ambivalents and do not realize there is any clash of opposing methodologies. Consequently, they will probably say 'It is a game' and leave it at that. The following account of THE COMMONS GAME is fairly typical:

> Players were directed to accumulate the maximum number of points. The player with the highest number of points received $5. The words 'win' or 'winner' were never used by the game directors. Greed and curiosity to get the commons up or down played significant roles in determining the teams' results. No goals were set at the beginning of the game; however, they tended to evolve during the game. Occasionally, players forgot about the commons and only 'played the game'. Titles of essays by the students reflect the confusion, frustration and complexity of dealing with commons property as shown in the following examples: 1. Can Humanity Survive? 2. Can We

Save the Commons? 3. Common Cents (Or Don't Be Petty With Your Cash). 4. Managing Commons Property Resources: The Simulation and The Real World. (Kirts, Tumeo and Sinz 1991)

Not only is this account full of contradictions, the facilitators seem unsure of the deceit. The terminology is gaming, the intention is simulation, the signals are inconsistent. The facilitators scrupulously avoid using the words 'win' and 'winner' in the briefing yet announce a prize of five dollars for the winner. This real money is an addition by the facilitators, not part of the original event. Real-world rewards are incompatible with the simulation mode.

No goals are set, suggesting that the facilitators were dimly aware that deceit might be involved. But who needs goals with $5 on the table for the person with the highest number of points? The only way to ensure winning the $5 (or a share in the prize) is to play the green card and nothing else. Since the event is called a game and the participants are called 'players', there is nothing to indicate the trap: that it is discreditable to try to win the money. Some of the participants have been deceived into behaviour that was later criticized as reprehensible. No description is given of what actually happened. Presumably the simulation-mode participants who sacrificed their own immediate gains in an effort to raise the wealth of the commons were not overjoyed to see a 'winner' rewarded with real cash. Words such as greed, selfish, disloyal, and untrustworthy spring to mind and were probably uttered and supported by the facilitators. The finger of shame is pointed at the gamesters, particularly at the one who won the $5. The facilitators' criticism of those who 'only played the game' is not only manifestly unjust, it confirms that the facilitators were unaware of their own trickery.

Lacking the concepts, the facilitators (and participants) were lost in the usual semantic fog of an ambivalent. The word 'simulation' is nowhere mentioned, except in the title of an essay by one of the students who may have had a much clearer idea of what was happening than the facilitators. If the facilitators had not been bemused by their own terminology they would undoubtedly have apologized for their deceit in the debriefing and explained why it was necessary. They would have explained that what appeared to be a clash of ethics was actually a clash of methodologies. Certainly they would have tried to sooth hurt feelings and not add fuel to the flames. Also, their report would have avoided using 'game' as an umbrella-word and the authors would have taken care not to let its meaning slip from (a) a duty of players to try to win to (b) a duty of citizens to help the community.

I know the disturbance caused in the family of one experienced academic who ran THE COMMONS GAME with her children and told me how shocked the family had been that one daughter, who had argued most strongly in favour of supporting the commons, had been the one to play the green card. Instead of the family interpreting this as the difference between gaming behaviour and simulation behaviour the impression was that the episode gave an insight into the true nature of the daughter. As usual, no-one seemed to be aware that the event was an ambivalent, let alone a necessary ambivalent. The trickery went undetected.

The above analysis of PRISONER'S DILEMMA was to give examples that will be useful in tackling a far more complex event, STARPOWER, the best-known simulation in the world.

STARPOWER is widely regarded as being highly effective and has rarely been criticized, although it has rightly been regarded as dangerous. Garry Shirts says it should be used only by 'teachers who feel comfortable with vigorous reaction'. Those who have participated in it praise the insights not only into the behaviour of people with power but also the insights it revealed into their own behaviour. The result is often self-awareness. 'I never thought I would behave like that' is the tone of some remarks. Violence can occur.

> On one occasion a group of leftish liberal studies lecturers announced 'The name of the game is GRAB', and very shortly afterwards I was knocked to the floor and a pack of bonus cards torn from my hand. This was a pity – a meeting intended to show the hidden violence of our established society showed instead only the boorishness of some of its opponents. (Coleman 1977)

> A good example happened 15 years ago; the students still remember it. We were playing STARPOWER and a woman brought lollipop treats for the Circles on the second day of

play. The powerful Squares levied a tax and tried to take a lollipop away. The tax man was almost decked when he reached for the lollipop; but I stepped in the middle. We discussed this emotional incident in class, and they wrote about it in their journals, which helped them cool down. (Petranek 1994)

Incidentally, there is no provision in STARPOWER for the introduction of lollipops or any other real-world rewards. As seen in the case of PRISONER'S DILEMMA, real-world rewards are an intrusion incompatible with the methodology of simulations.

STARPOWER began life as a routine, black-versus-white simulation in which the 'blacks', white students in real life, jumped on tables and demanded their rights. Everyone was pleased except for Garry Shirts, who was dismayed by the play acting and the failure of the event to explore the deprivations and discrimination suffered by the have-nots in a society. So he moved the event into the abstract. He allocated coloured tokens, unequally, to represent wealth and after a few trading sessions divided the participants into Squares, Circles and Triangles, depending on their wealth. Trading continued until the facilitator announced that the wealthiest group, the Squares, had been so successful they could, in consultation with other groups if they wished, change the rules.

What usually happens is that the Squares seek to change the rules to consolidate or increase their own wealth and as a result the Circles become annoyed and apprehensive while the Triangles become abusive, truculent, disinterested, and apathetic. The first time I participated in STARPOWER the facilitator strode into the centre of the room. 'There,' he cried, pointing to the Triangles, 'there is your revolution for you!'

Few people have attempted to analyse what goes on in STARPOWER and fewer have criticized the design of the event. By far the most interesting, and devastating, criticism is by Margaret Gredler in her book *Designing and Evaluating Games and Simulations: A Process Approach*. In Gredler's view, STARPOWER has a major design fault and can result in serious personal consequences for the participants. She concluded that it should not be used. I shall argue that Gredler's analysis is extremely interesting but flawed. I quote several extracts from pages 130–3 in order to give a fairly full flavour of her argument. (Note: Although Gredler recognizes that games and simulations are psychologically incompatible, she uses 'exercise' as an umbrella-word to mean 'any interactive event'.)

STARPOWER is an ingenious exercise in that conflict between the groups is established. However, the exercise contains a design flaw that generates undesirable effects when implemented.

The design of empathy/insight simulations should be consistent with two basic requirements. First, participants should not be misled about the nature of the situation nor tricked in any way into executing behaviours that are later criticized. Second, like other simulations, empathy/insight simulations are not games and care should be taken that participants do not view them as games. STARPOWER, however, violates both requirements. First, participants are told they are participating in a game and that the three highest scores will win. When given the opportunity to make the rules, the Squares do so in a way that ensures that three of their group will be the winners. There is no difference between this behaviour and the behaviour of bankrupting one's friends in Monopoly. Both actions are entirely legitimate in a game situation.

However, the behaviour of the Squares is extrapolated into the real world as though the Squares were not playing a game. They have, in other words, been tricked. In fact, the Director's Instructions include the statement that the Squares sometimes have difficulty in admitting that they abused their power (Shirts 1969, page 18). They are quite correct – their behaviour was appropriate for the game they believed they were playing.

The Director's Instructions also describe the concepts that typically emerge from the post-simulation discussion. Two of the concepts are '1. Each of us may be more vulnerable to the temptation to abuse powers than we realise' and '2. To change behaviour, it may be necessary to change the system in which that behaviour occurs'. In other words, participants have been asked to judge the Squares' game behaviour as though it were real-world behaviour. Participants are not sophisticated enough to understand the difference between games and simulations and thus do not question the transfer.

A more serious problem, however, is that issues of trust may be raised: Susan (a Triangle) may wonder if Diane (a Square) is entirely trustworthy. Hard feelings generated by the exercise may persist into the educational or work setting.

Setting aside for the moment the design flaws within the exercise, what post-simulation decisions are to be undertaken in a different way as a result of participation in the exercise?

Gredler goes on to examine, one by one, several desirable behavioural changes (such as become more vigilant citizens) and concludes that most of these aims are not clear and those that are clear would be better achieved by a different type of interactive event.

Gredler's analysis is admirable for her focus on damage to the participants. The references to Susan and Diane are very helpful examples. The distress is typical of what can happen in an ambivalent. Her conclusion that facilitators should not use the event follows mainly from her view that participants should not be misled about the nature of the situation nor tricked in any way into executing behaviours that are later criticized. However, this runs two points together, trickery and criticism. Yet, the first does not require the second. Indeed, if the facilitator was aware that the participants had been tricked this should have been explained in the debriefing and the criticism should not have been made.

The major flaw in the analysis is that Gredler seems not to notice that the event is in three parts. She seems unaware of the significance of the intrusion of the real world at the point where the facilitator gives the Squares the power to change the rules. At this point the so-called 'game' stops – there is no trading. Everyone discusses the situation. Consequently, the event has three separate and distinct periods:

1. Trading sessions
2. Intrusion of real life, from the facilitator
3. Subsequent action, with the Squares as legislators or possibly as game designers.

Let us look at each period in turn and decide the most likely category of methodology.

1. Trading sessions

On the face of it, the most likely category for the trading sessions is an economic and social simulation. Unlike games, but like real life, participants do not start with equal wealth. As trading progresses, the rich stay rich and the poor stay poor. The social aspect of the simulation is enhanced by the rule that trading pairs must have physical contact while trading. If the facilitator called the event a simulation and referred to the participants as participants then it is likely that the trading sessions would fall into the simulation category with the participants taking the role of traders and behaving professionally. However, this is highly unlikely to occur since Shirts refers to the event as a game and establishes a scoring mechanism. Moreover, most facilitators are addicted to gaming terminology and are likely to call the event a game and refer to the participants as players. The more intelligent and experienced participants are likely to spot the discrepancy between the label and the event, but for the inexperienced, the gullible and also the highly competitively-minded, the trading sessions are likely to be played as a game, with no intrusive thoughts of real life. For these participants they are in the isolated world of game. In such cases Gredler is right, the facilitator and Garry Shirts have tricked at least some of the participants into behaving like players.

2. Intrusion of real life, from the facilitator

This period cannot possibly come into the category of a game. First, the facilitator is not a player but a dictator from outside the event. Second, no game is in progress, it is a time-out to discuss the rules. Third, in no game is it remotely conceivable that the side who are winning should suddenly have the power to move the goalposts since games are designed to be fair and offer equal opportunities. Yet, in real life power is often granted to the successful and those with power sometimes change the rules in their own favour. In my opinion, period two is a stroke of genius by Garry Shirts.

3. Subsequent action with the Squares as legislators or, possibly, game designers

What usually happens is that the three groups meet separately to discuss the situation. The Squares may or may not start changing the rules. Probably they see themselves as legislators, or possibly, they think of themselves as game designers. Certainly, the Circles and Triangles are likely to realize that they are governed by the Squares and they, particularly the Triangles, will dislike the change of status. Previously they may have been poor but their poverty was due to Garry Shirts, aided and abetted by the facilitator. Now their fate rests with the Squares. No one at this stage can possibly believe the event is a game rather than a simulation. For one thing there are no rules, they are suspended awaiting development. Sometimes there is a half-hearted attempt to restart trading but usually the event ends in chaos and protest. The Squares tend to walk tall, the Circles tend to be bemused or resentful and the Triangles tend to slouch and become either apathetic or aggressive.

In the light of this analysis of the three periods let us see what Gredler alleges. She says that bankrupting one's friends in MONOPOLY is in the same category of behaviour as changing the trading rules in STARPOWER. But this is not the case. First, one does not try to bankrupt one's friends in MONOPOLY, one tries to win the game – it is not betrayal of friendship, nor is it personal greed, it is a duty. Second, redesigning a game is a completely different activity to playing a game. It is as if, in MONOPOLY, it was suddenly announced during a game that the first person to have built an hotel could change the rules.

Gredler suggests that sophistication is required to distinguish between the activities of playing a game and redesigning the rules. Common experience suggests this is not true. Even young children enjoy not only playing games but designing and redesigning their own games. They pay great attention to fairness and justice. 'That's not fair' is a common protest by young children who are designing games or playing games.

It is important to look at what actually happens, or what is likely to happen in an event. Imagine a hypothetical trading event in which the following remarks were made:

Diane: I offer two whites for one of your golds.
Susan: It's not fair that you start with more golds than I
          have.

Diane's remark is within the event and facilitates action, whether
the game is a game, a simulation, role play or an exercise. Susan's
remark, on the other hand, halts the action and starts a real-life
discussion about the rules. Whereas Diane is inside the event,
Susan is outside it, judging it, criticizing it.

However, let us grant the supposition that the Squares rewrote
the rules to their own advantage while believing their rule-
changing to be part of the 'game' as distinct from outside the
'game'. In this case, their behaviour would be highly reprehensible
and unethical, a denial of the basic ethical concept of gaming. In
real life, people can get killed for fixing games. In any case, any
attempt by a winning team to fix rules in favour of the winning
team is likely to be unproductive since no-one else would play.
However, the Squares could argue that it was the facilitator who
introduced the unfairness by giving them, and them alone, rule-
changing powers and that they were only doing what they were
expected to do: change the rules to make sure they won the game.
But in this case they had moved out of the world of gaming into
the real world of expected behaviour and the 'good student'
syndrome. Not only were they not in a game, they were not in a
simulation. In a simulation they had to accept their role, to act in
the best interest of that role, be it as legislator or game designer
and to justify their actions on these grounds. But here they were
not in role, they were themselves trying to produce expected
behaviour. Their motivation was politeness, compliance and
respect for the teacher or trainer. So to argue: 'We did what we
thought you wanted' is real-world intrusion.

However, suppose that the Squares realized that whatever the
category of the event when it began it was now a simulation in
which they were in the role of governors and the others were the
governed. Greed is possible but not necessary. I participated in
STARPOWER in Denmark when the Squares decided to change the
rules so that wealth was divided equally. Even if the Squares
decide to protect their wealth, or possibly increase it, this is not
necessarily personal greed. For one thing, it is not a real-world

situation with real money. It is an imaginary, simulated scenario in which they are citizens and their motives might be unselfish. For example, they could envisage they had families and wished to preserve the existing trading rules, not for personal gain, but because of a heartfelt duty to their family. It would be cynical to assume that such participants were hypocrites. There are plenty of precedents they could cite from the real world of people in power using that power to protect the interests of their families, friends and communities. However, if they were merely imitating the real world then the event for them would not be a simulation, it would be mimicry or play acting. In a simulation it is up to the participants to take their own decisions for their own reasons and not to imitate other people's decisions.

Crucial to Gredler's criticism is the accusation of deceit. But wherein lies this trickery? It might at first appear that the deceit occurs when the facilitator gives the Squares the power to rewrite the rules. But no deceit is involved here, it is simply blatant unfairness and is perfectly obvious to everyone.

Gredler says that in the debriefing the participants have been asked to judge the Squares' game-behaviour as though it were real-world behaviour.

> The behaviour of the Squares is extrapolated into the real world as though the Squares were not playing a game. They have, in other words, been tricked. The Director's Instructions include the statement that the Squares sometimes have difficulty in admitting that they abused their power (Shirts, 1969, page 18). They are quite correct – their behaviour was appropriate for the game they believed they were playing.

But Gredler is referring to the rule-changing session, not to the Squares' behaviour in the trading session, the 'game'. As argued above, they are not playing a game when rule-changing. They are in (a) a simulation with the role of legislators or (b) a simulation with the role of game designers or (c) a real-life situation in which they are trying to please authority by producing expected behaviour. This brings us to perhaps the most crucial criticism that Gredler makes, people getting hurt.

A more serious problem, however, is that issues of trust may be raised: Susan (a Triangle) may wonder if Diane (a Square) is entirely trustworthy. Hard feelings generated by the exercise may persist into the educational or work setting.

This argument about trust does not make sense according to Gredler's own analysis. Her hypothesis is that the participants have been tricked into believing the event is a game. But issues of friendship and trust are not gaming issues. Players do not expect their friends on the other team to show them any favours. On the contrary, they would become upset if they thought their friends were not really trying. Even young children protest: 'Oh Daddy, you let me win'. Gredler's analysis would make perfect sense if applied to the session of PRISONER'S DILEMMA mentioned earlier. In such an event Susan might say: 'I thought you were my best friend. I stuck by you but you let me down. I trusted you but you betrayed me. By saying that I was guilty, you got off lightly and I go to prison for a long time. I know it is not real but I shall never speak to you again.'

To quote again from Liebrand (see page 20):

Comments such as 'If you defect on the rest of us, you're going to live with it for the rest of your life' were not uncommon. Nor was it unusual for people to wish to leave the experimental building by the back door, to claim that they did not wish to see the 'sons of bitches' who double-crossed them, to become extremely angry at other subjects, or to become tearful.

Gredler misses the point about STARPOWER. During the trading sessions, Susan is unlikely to have any animosity against her friend whether she thinks the event is a game or a simulation. Yet, Susan cannot help noticing that Diane started rich and stayed rich, whereas she started poor and remains poor. She does not blame Diane or the other Squares for their wealth, although she may envy them. What she does resent is the inequality, unfairness and injustice of the so-called game. The fact that the facilitator calls it a game may damp down her resentment since the event might be 'only a game', of no real consequence and supposedly played for fun. However, the feeling of being hard done by is hugely magnified when the facilitator gives the power of legislation to the Squares on the untruthful assertion that they have shown themselves to be the best traders. The lie and the granting of legislator powers is an intrusion from real life, an episode of a different category from game, simulation, role play or exercise.

As pointed out earlier, this is not a matter of sophisticated semantics in distinguishing between games and simulations. It is a matter of real-world experience. Even children are quick to pick up not only what is allowed in games and real life, but also who is a legitimate rule-maker or rule-changer (older brothers and sisters, parents, teachers, committees, legislatures, etc).

Child A: It is my bat and ball so you have to get me out three times.

Children B, C, D: You can't change the rules.

STARPOWER is a simulation that starts life disguised as a game, or trading simulation. When the Squares receive legislative power everything changes fundamentally, including attitudes and emotions. No longer a player, Diane is a governor and a legislator, or a game-designer. Even if Diane and the other Squares feel benevolent and wish to give the Triangles more wealth they are likely to appear smug in the eyes of the recipients of their gifts. However generous and altruistic Diane might be, she cannot evade the possibility that her magnanimity may be rebuffed and she herself regarded as playing Lady Bountiful. I have been in sessions of STARPOWER when the visiting Squares offering favours and benefits to the Triangles were received with the utmost contempt and hostility. 'Who do you think you are?' was the tone of the responses.

Gredler could be even more critical about potential damage to friendships – damage is not all one-way. Diane can also be taken aback by Susan's behaviour even before the Squares have started to discuss their legislative policy. Susan is now no longer a player but a protester. Her face is no longer passive or smiling but animated with suspicion and dislike as she looks at the Squares. But why? Diane and her fellow Squares have done nothing wrong and may be willing to redistribute their wealth. In fact, Diane might be surprised and dismayed to find that Susan, whom she thought was her best friend, is suddenly revealed as petulant, bad-tempered and unreasonable. Susan may be looking at her with dislike. Susan might even have turned into a street-corner agitator before her very eyes.

Gredler also seems to limit her hypothetical damage to participants, thus missing the likely damage to the facilitator. This can be very serious. The participants, however lacking they may be in the terminology of such events, all know who set up the situation – it was the facilitator. They also know, or suspect, that the facilitator was lying by giving power to the Squares on the pretence that they were the more skilful traders. They will almost certainly be aware of the original unequal distribution of wealth and the subsequent ineffectiveness of ways to increase wealth (apart from theft (Coleman, 1977) see page 29). The facilitator is unlikely to apologize for (a) setting up a rich–poor trading situation originally, (b) giving rule-changing power to the winning group, and (c) lying about the reason for doing so.

Unfortunately, the facilitator, instead of confessing, is likely to make matters worse by pointing to alleged personal moral failings – to the Squares who 'sometimes have difficulty in admitting that they abused their power'. Not only is this grossly unfair, it damages the accuser as well as the accused. Sooner or later the participants will discuss their hurt feelings and work out who was to blame. This may never surface in the classroom, either from a 'good-student' attitude or a fear of the consequences of protest. The facilitator may be surprised by subsequent behaviour: 'I thought Susan was a good student, but now she seems uncooperative and unfriendly. I expect it is something to do with her personal life.' In such ways the wagons of concealment, hurt and misunderstanding roll on.

Yet none of this damage need occur if the facilitator was not blinded by gaming concepts and actually looked at what was really taking place and not seek to blame the participants. Even if the Squares did legislate in their own interests, this is no evidence of greed. It may be greed. But only Diane knows if she was feeling greedy and uncaring. Her innocence should be presumed. It may be greed. But only Diane knows if she was feeling greedy and uncaring. Her innocence should be presumed. In any case, to focus the debriefing on criticizing the behaviour of the Squares is not only grossly unfair, it misses the most important real-life parallel.

39

What happens after the changes are made? Is there blood on the streets? Changes made for economic reasons often bring social and political consequences. 'There is your revolution for you!' cried the facilitator, pointing to the behaviour of the Triangles. He was right, he was pointing to real-life consequences.

This analysis has followed Gredler in concentrating on two hypothetical participants – Diane a Square and Susan a Triangle. But in doing so it has omitted mention of a safeguard introduced by Shirts to reduce the danger to individuals. Unlike many events, STARPOWER does not contain the instruction 'Pick a leader'. This is quite deliberate. Shirts knows that in practice it is easier to make a scapegoat of an individual than of a group. Many ambivalents set up leaders and entrap them.

It would be regrettable if such a brilliant event as STARPOWER were struck from the schedules. Gredler says that participants cannot distinguish between a game and a simulation. However, participants should not be underestimated. In the hours, days or months following such a memorable event they can often work things out and may have a clearer idea of what went on than the facilitator. However, it is unfortunate if facilitators run this, and other ambivalents, without knowing what they are doing and cause unwitting damage to participants and to themselves.

As stated earlier, compared with real life, one of the virtues of simulations is that they are safe. This description does not apply to ambivalents.

Chapter 2

Simulations for teaching and training

WAR AND BUSINESS

The first organized use of simulations is usually attributed to the Prussian army in the nineteenth century. It occurred for behavioural reasons. The Prussians had been dissatisfied with the recruitment of officers, and decided that the interview and the pen and paper tests were not enough. Consequently, they devised simulations to test behaviour. Instead of asking 'How would you cope with situation X?' the idea was to place the person in that situation, as far as was practical and desirable, and see what happened.

The idea was later taken up by the British army. All sorts of behavioural situations were devised in which the candidates had roles – officer, survivor, agent, engineer. They were tests which revealed varying degrees of ingenuity, cooperation, leadership, courage and other aspects of military life. Some were non-interactive simulations in which individual participants had to tackle a situation without help or cooperation, but most were interactive simulations involving teams. The simulation technique was also widely introduced into army training

The differences between these simulations and written tests affected not only the participants but also the assessors. For example, the assessors of a test paper usually wait until the end of the test and then check the result. But with simulations the observation covers the whole of the activities. Behaviour is very much a matter of process rather than product, and assessors become very involved in behavioural tests because they are looking at living people, not lifeless paper.

In the United States after the outbreak of the Second World War the military were faced with the problem of how to recruit spies. The original plan involved the recruitment of criminals on the grounds that dirty work required criminal experience. This policy of recruitment resulted in several disasters in the field, and a change in recruitment techniques was deemed desirable. One option which was considered was to advertise for people willing to undertake dangerous work, but this was rejected on the grounds that it would bring in a flood of macho posturing cranks and psychopaths. At that time an American officer returned from Sandhurst military college and described the British methods of simulations. This was taken up by the Americans. Likely officers and men were seconded to a test centre organized by the OSS, the Office of Strategic Services, for recruitment tests lasting several days. After a good deal of trial and error, a system was evolved whereby each candidate had to adopt a cover story – name, birthplace, schooling, career, etc – which were not his own, but related to things he knew about. All were instructed that they must stick to their cover stories at all times, except in condition 'X' which would be announced formally by one of the staff. At various times, particularly after failing a test, individual candidates would be interviewed in a relaxed atmosphere by a member of staff who would say something on the lines of 'Don't worry about it, few people get through that test, but I suppose you have had tough experiences in the past'. At this point some candidates blurted out their true experiences and revealed their actual background, thus breaking cover.

One particularly frustrating task was to take on the role of a supervisor who had to erect a construction by giving directions to two 'helpers'. The 'helpers' were members of staff who would obey orders to place the bits and pieces in position, but if the instructions were ambiguous they would do the wrong thing, and at times they would stop and offer 'helpful' suggestions. Sometimes a candidate would strike the helpers and drop out of the course there and then. (OSS 1948)

Subsequently, the OSS experiences were used as a basis for simulations in business and industry in the United States. As was pointed out, choosing a manager is no different in principle from choosing a spy. All that is needed is to see what sort of behaviour is desirable and undesirable in the job, and then devise appropriate simulations. These business assessment procedures were generally known as assessment centres, although sometimes there was no centre as such, and the assessment was carried out at whatever location was the most suitable. (Moses 1977)

In recent years there has been an intersecting of army and business simulations. At one time all simulations in the army were military action simulations, but recently management simulations have been introduced in Britain, West Germany and some other countries. Army officers participate in simulations which deal with such matters as the design and procurement of weapons, and participants may take the role of officials in the Ministry of Defence, commercial companies which manufacture weapons, and so on. The reason for this use of management simulations is military awareness of the growing importance of logistics.

Although the word 'game' is used from time to time in both the armed forces and in business it may now be on the decline. There are operations rooms and assessment centres rather than games rooms and games centres. The usual words are exercise, simulation, test, assessment. With the armed forces the word 'game' is usually avoided. In the British army there are what is known as TEWTs, Tactical Exercises Without Troops, not Tactical Games Without Troops. And when one country informs another that it intends to hold military manoeuvres near its borders, the phrase used is military exercises, not military games.

In business, the label 'games' is still popular among top management, and the reason for this is far from clear. Perhaps managers like the idea of playing games, or maybe the word signifies status, since the terminology for lower-ranking staff is usually 'exercise' or 'simulation'. The phrase 'management game' is fairly widely used, and, perhaps significantly, there is no equivalent phrase for the rest of the staff. There are signs that gaming terminology, even among managers, is being replaced by more appropriate professional labels. However, the phrases 'war games' and 'business games' are still popular in the media. They are the terminology of the headline writers and the television and film makers. Many authors and simulation designers also are attracted to the word 'game', perhaps because it indicates a 'fun' element, and they probably believe, perhaps mistakenly, that it helps sell the product.

The argument is not that genuine business games and war games do not exist. They do, and in plentiful numbers, as can be seen by walking into a games shop. They involve players, the aim is to win, and the object of participation is enjoyment. A characteristic is that they can be played many times, whereas it is most unusual for a specific simulation (or exercise, or informal drama) to be rerun with the same group.

War and business are useful examples of areas in which simulations have been developed, but simulations are also widely used in recruitment and training for all jobs which require behavioural skills. They are an established part of police training (crime and accident simulations), air transport (flight deck simulators), the medical profession (simulated injuries), the law (mock trials). The terminology of gaming tends to be avoided at the professional level. Moreover, the aims of the simulations are related mainly to the process rather than the end results, so the observational data includes all the muddles, misunderstandings and false starts. The first thoughts as well as the second thoughts are part of the evidence.

EDUCATION AND TRAINING

Simulations are used far more in training than in education. In training the emphasis is on the practical, on decision-making, on communication skills and on doing a job. If the job requires behavioural skills, then simulation is an obvious technique to employ. In education, on the other hand, the emphasis is not on behaviour but on the learning of facts. A general distinction is that training is particularly concerned with the process, whereas education is more concerned with the 'product'.

A clear example of the 'product' approach can be seen in the educational system in the United States. It is geared to results, far more than in most other countries. This arises partly because of the way education is funded in the United States, with great importance attached to the end product in order to achieve grants and other financial benefits.

A major consequence is that the end product tends to be clearly defined and measurable so that success and failure can be reflected in statistics. Numbers are regarded as being more impressively objective than words, descriptions and opinions. Since statistics of measurable achievements have such an important status it follows that priority must be given to tests which reveal easily quantifiable results. And this in turn leads to emphasis on testing the recall of facts, rather than the response to open questions. The consequence of concentrating on examinations with closed questions leads to the encouragement of didactic teaching and programmed learning. Since the justification for the American system is the end result it follows that it is essential to specify precisely the nature of the task, for without clear objectives there can be no way of telling whether the right results have been achieved. Once the task has been defined the system requires that pupils and students should be tested, usually frequently tested, to make sure that they are on course. Given the nature of this system it is not surprising that the favoured method of instruction is step-by-step learning, and that the dominant educational psychology is behaviourist with emphasis on the frequent reinforcement of correct responses.

This step-by-step method of advancing towards precisely defined objectives influences American simulation design. For example, Richard Duke of the University of Michigan, advocates nine detailed and sequential steps in design (1979). Duke, who always uses the word 'game' calls his first step 'Specification for Game Design'. He says

> Game architects need a blueprint composed of carefully delineated, detailed game specifications. At the outset, they need to conform to a plan, providing a clear, concise picture of the product to be created.

It seems that the word 'game' changes its meaning as it crosses the Atlantic. In the United States, it acquires educational and training connotations. The two national American games, baseball and

American football, have far more trainer control than soccer or cricket. American football, for example, has frequent time-outs to allow the coaches to communicate strategy. Professional teams have books of a hundred or more tactics. The word 'game' is more frequently used as a metaphor in the United States than in Europe, probably because it is closely associated with education and training. A 'game plan' refers to a far more controlled sequence of events on the American football field than in the case of soccer. So the word 'game' in the United States has a kind of academic association which it does not possess in Europe where games are usually relegated to the playing fields and game shops. Many teachers would not risk running a game in the classroom for fear of seeming too frivolous.

In Britain, there is more emphasis on the importance of process. For a long time, British primary schools have been centres of simulations, activities of a 'professional' nature where the children behave like architects, designers, artists, and shopkeepers – and use simulations. This is sometimes misleadingly referred to as 'play'. In the field of foreign-language teaching, British educationalists were mainly responsible for the Communicative Movement of the 1970s, based on the premise that languages should not be taught for their own sake but in order that they may be used, and that language in use means language in communication. Whereas the previous didactic teaching had concentrated almost exclusively on vocabulary, grammar, and pronunciation, the Communicative Movement shifted the emphasis to oral and behavioural skills. In its philosophy, psychology, and methodology the Communicative Movement formed a creative whole, changing attitudes and practices of teachers in many countries. It was concerned with processes rather than products, active learning rather than passive, and interaction between students rather than a purely teacher-dominated approach. Simulations have long been an accepted part of tuition and sometimes of assessment. This movement has influenced teaching and training generally, although the amount of group work and simulations used in educational and business establishments varies a great deal.

However, the comparison between a British 'process' philosophy and an American 'product' philosophy in education and training is not as sharp as the above might imply. In the United

States there are powerful voices which criticize the frequent testing of fact learning and in Britain there are plenty of teachers who rely exclusively on direct instruction.

PERSONAL DEVELOPMENT

Simulations have advantages over most other methodologies when dealing with personal development.

- Unlike real life, the environment in a simulation is 'safe'; people can experiment and develop. In real life careers can ossify, habits can form, obligations can constrain. Simulations, on the other hand, provide wide-ranging job opportunities within functional (professional) roles – as distinct from roles intended for play acting, mimicry, imitation.
- Simulations, unlike most role plays, are not 'performed'. No one has to act out a role. There is no audience, unless it is part of the simulation. The job, functions, duties and responsibilities in a simulation mean that personal development is not hindered by stage-fright. Participants remain themselves and develop their own skills, personalities and experiences without mimicry. No one has to assume emotions or pretend. Whereas role play can be a useful tool in therapy sessions, role play used in education and training can seem an undesirable invasion of privacy to some participants. To be picked on to act is not everyone's cup of tea. Simulations are not play acting, but they can be used in group therapy specifically to help the personal development of patients in the context of functional roles. For the facilitator (psychologist) simulations have the great advantage of providing a non-threatening environment in which the psychologist is peripheral and can observe behaviour and assess personal development. By granting the participants personal (and professional) job responsibilities simulations can encourage self-confidence – often lacking in people who are psychologically disturbed.
- Unlike games, which are essentially competitive and rarely involve much talk ('Two hearts', 'Your turn'), simulations allow a full range of behaviours in the context of personal

development, cooperation, empathy, and discussion. Moreover, instead of a materialistic world of scoring and winning, simulations are ideal for human and ethical qualities. The situations are related to real life and its customs and conventions, even in abstract events such as STARPOWER. Games exist in a self-contained magic kingdom of their own rules.

- Exercises are essentially problem-solving activities geared to finding satisfactory answers, whereas simulations give authority related to the role. The people in a simulation are not problem-solvers as such, they are journalists, doctors, or business executives, although their job will almost certainly include problem-solving. They have power. There is no teacher or trainer in the newsroom, the consulting room or the boardroom. In fact, the participants occasionally use their powers to reject the problem the facilitator expected them to discuss. Supposing the intended problem was a shortage of paper clips in a company and the facilitator expected a discussion about how many to order and at what price. Supposing, however, that the documents suggested theft, lack of motivation and inadequate supervision, then the managers might decide to tackle the major questions and leave the ordering of paper clips to the office equipment department.

- Games rarely involve much talk. Chess and Scrabble can be played in silence. Formalized talk occurs in bridge, 'one diamond', 'pass'. In Monopoly the required talk is restricted to matters of game procedure, announcing decisions. There is relatively more required talk in quiz 'games', including Trivial Pursuit, but this is restricted to answering factual questions. In any case, quizzes are competitions rather than games. There is no significant difference in format between a general knowledge quiz, an 'amateur-night' contest and an international competition for the best choir: the contestants are performers, not players, and there are no strategies, tactics or interactive moves. In contrast to games, simulations usually encourage (and require) talk – interviews, presentations, explanations, suggestions, summings-up, discussions and debates.

- Simulations are ideal for revealing human and ethical qualities, all part of the concept of personal development. They can involve cooperation, sympathy, help, empathy and also deal with ethical dilemmas, in contrast to the materialistic gaming world where the prime duty is to win and the only ethic is the concept of fair play.

● Simulations are related to real life in some form or another. This applies to abstract simulations such as STARPOWER and also to simulations where the rules or conventions are deliberately the opposite to those in real life in order to provoke comparisons during the debriefing. The real life connection allows the facilitator to use an experiential simulation as an analogy, reflection, or metaphor in a variety of situations that have a bearing on personal development. Personality development in games tends to be more restricted: the usefulness of cooperation and team spirit in team games, the virtue of being a 'good loser' in all games, etc.

The argument here is not that games, role plays and exercises do not help personal development but that simulations offer the opportunity of increased personal understanding – for both participants and facilitator. Moreover, there is one aspect of simulations which rarely occurs with the other methodologies, the debriefing. The debriefing, as will be dealt with later, does not automatically mean that the facilitator stands in front of the class, asking questions. If the simulation involves groups, each group could take it in turn to make a presentation. For example, if the simulation were a foreign-affairs event, then each country could first discuss how to present their findings: who should say what, then make a joint presentation revealing what was contained in their secret documents, what their aims were and what they did. Such debriefings offer plenty of opportunity for personal development.

Another argument in favour of using simulations to stimulate personal development is that simulations often embrace values as well as communication skills. The values can be ethical, aesthetic, personal and even, on occasions, religious. Often the values are implicit rather than explicit, or arise accidentally, or are private. If, in a simulation involving a business meeting, a participant thinks:

He is completely wrong about that. But if I point it out it will hurt his feelings. On the other hand he was somewhat discourteous to Mary and probably deserves to be taken down a peg or two. However, I should not act out of malice. Never-theless, I feel I have a duty to the company to point out the inefficiency of what he is proposing. If I am honest with myself then perhaps I should ...

Such thoughts (ideas, considerations, views, values, feelings) are private and involve ethics and value judgements. As can be seen in the last chapter, simulations can have a deep personal influence that can escape notice. In STARPOWER, only Diane knows if she was being greedy. Only she knows her thoughts and emotions. Did she feel superior because she was a Square? Did she feel condescension to the Triangles or think that, since they shuffled around and looked displeased, they somehow mattered less? In particular, how did she feel about her friend Susan, who was a Triangle? Similarly, Susan is the only person who knows her feelings towards the Squares and to Diane in particular. Were her thoughts ungenerous or unjustified? Did either of the two participants afterwards think to themselves 'I never thought I could behave, think, or feel like that'? Such thoughts can be catalysts. They can be as influential as they are private. Nor is the self-awareness confined to the event and the debriefing. Weeks or months later, recollections of such a powerful event can trigger changes in personal, behavioural and ethical values. Because facilitators are, for the most part, unaware of what has happened these profound changes usually go unreported.

SOCIAL AND CULTURAL

Social and cultural simulations form a large category. This is not surprising in view of the profound effect which simulations can have on personal development in a social and cultural context.

On an official level, simulations are a long-standing method of research into cultural and foreign relations and are widely used by institutions to explore options of policy. Some of these simulations continue for days or weeks. In format they are similar to military simulations, but concentrate on social and cultural forces.

Many of these studies showed large differences between cultures in bargaining behaviour. For example, in numerous experiments with adults it was found that they continued the pattern found in children's games. The softer bargainer adjusted his or her moves to match the opponent's tougher stance, often producing impasse. Druckman (1994) says that simulations 'can remove the cultural blinkers that impeded effective interaction with people of different cultural, social, or ethnic backgrounds, or from different departments, companies, or countries'.

On a social, as distinct from an inter-cultural, level, simulations are widely used in universities, schools and companies to reveal the forces at work in communities – bureaucracy, caring, power, intolerance, compassion, law, ethics. STARPOWER is an example, seemingly about bits of coloured paper involving groups labelled by geometric shapes, it uses these superficial abstractions to reveal economic, social, cultural, and political power. Reading a book or seeing a video about power is no substitute for experiencing it.

Here are other examples to illustrate the wide diversity of social and cultural simulations.

TALKING ROCKS was written by Robert F Vernon, an expert on prehistoric petroglyphs and pictographs, with help and advice from Garry Shirts. It is a good example of simulations which are both simple and sophisticated, suitable for children and adults. In the manual Vernon intimates that the main aim (and perhaps the original aim) is to attack the stereotypes of 'primitive people' and 'noble savages' and instead allow participants to appreciate just how sophisticated and ingenious our early ancestors were. But with this aim the simulation could have been merely a teaching tool, perhaps based on documentary evidence of petroglyphs and pictographs. Perhaps the participants could have the role of research workers who had to produce a report for their university department or the school magazine. Some authors might have added forms for the participants to fill in to reveal how much they had learned. Instead, the participants are part of pre-history. They are the Eagle People who move from site to site, leaving messages for those who come later. Each camp site has an easel or board with large sheets of paper for drawing the messages. When a group arrives at a camp site the facilitator gives them a card which shows what they know. For example: 'Travel south across the desert from here for two days. You will find a river. Follow the river to the west for half a day and you will find a huge pasture'.

This has to be drawn as a survival message for the next group. No words or letters are allowed. No modern symbols can be used. For example, the skull and crossbones cannot be used to indicate poison; an arrow cannot be used to indicate north; the words and letters related to compass points must not be used. (The compass has not been invented.) There must be no talking between groups and the cards handed out by the facilitator must be kept secret from other groups.

Groups of Eagle People move simultaneously from one site to the next. The Manual shows a diagram for five sites and if the simulation takes place in one room, the participants are asked to speak softly to avoid other groups overhearing their discussion. There are twelve cards to be transcribed into 'survival messages'. When a group arrives at a campsite, it has to work out the meaning of the drawings left by the previous group and then devise their own drawings from another card given to them by the facilitator. What tends to happen is that as the groups move from site to site, they start to develop a common vocabulary, picking up ways of drawing directions and indicating food or danger.

What the Manual does not point out is the danger of using gaming terminology. If the facilitator introduces TALKING ROCKS as a game rather than as a simulation there is an immediate contradiction. The groups are supposed to help each other, not compete with each other. If it were a game, it would be a contest to see which group survived the longest.

The most popular social and cultural simulation is Garry Shirts' BAFA BAFA. It consists of two cultural groups, the Alpha and the Beta, and they are briefed separately and given practice in their own customs and, in the case of Beta, their own language. The briefing for the Alpha group explains that they are warm, friendly, and patriarchal. The Beta group is 'foreign-speaking', materialistic, and task-oriented. The artifacts of the simulation include trading cards and visitors' badges. A group from each culture visits the other culture and reports back. Further visits take place when visitors can test the hypotheses brought back by earlier visitors. One of the rules of the simulation is that the participants are not allowed to ask about the rules of the culture they visit, they must depend on their own observations. Garry Shirts discusses the question of what happens in the debriefing if participants complain that they should have been allowed to ask direct questions about the rules.

'If I could have asked about the rules, I would have been able to do O.K. in the other culture', is the way belief may be expressed. Maybe, but asking questions in the simulation may be less like the 'real world' than one would think. Often members of the other culture speak a language or a dialect the visitor doesn't understand and so it is difficult to ask or answer questions. Moreover, we are often reluctant to ask questions about ways of behaving for fear of being rude. It's hard to ask why one does something without seeming to question the validity of that behaviour. Furthermore, many actions which are culturally determined are not evident to the person in that culture. Few Americans, for instance, are aware that they space themselves approximately 18 inches apart when standing in a group, or the conditions and circumstances which govern the amount of time it is appropriate for them to look another person directly in the eye.

BAFA BAFA has been used in many contexts. In the United States, it is more or less standard practice in training courses for institutions and in the armed forces for staff who go on overseas assignments. Like most other good interactive simulations it reveals aspects not only of other people's behaviour but also of one's own. One feels the frustrations of trying to understand a different culture and also, perhaps, a certain smug reassurance in one's own culture. What often emerges is that the participants are surprised and puzzled that behaviour X or custom Y can have quite different meanings, depending on one's own culture. For example, what to an Alpha may seem like a pointless and random gesture can be a serious communication for someone in the Beta culture. To the Beta visitors the card-matching behaviour of the Alpha culture may seem trivial, but to the Alphas it is very meaningful. In theory the participants knew this already, but it was only book knowledge. Their experiences in BAFA BAFA made a profound and lasting impression.

CAPJEFOS - A SIMULATION OF VILLAGE DEVELOPMENT is designed by Cathy Greenblat. Villagers can choose to build a road but they have to give up social time (which exists within the event) and string together small safety pins. When it is 12 feet long the road is completed. On most runs of the simulation the road is unfinished. The leisure area is very comfortable. The Chief's role card includes the following:

You must diligently watch for threats to the community's traditions. Visitors to Capjefos should receive your approval before meeting with others. If you give them such approval, pin a star on their nametags.

What usually happens is that visitors without the Chief's star are treated somewhat differently from those with the star.

It is interesting that the title was changed – it was originally CAPJEFOS. THE VILLAGE DEVELOPMENT GAME. Clearly it is not a game, the participants are not players and there is no duty to 'win' – whatever that might mean in such circumstances. Real-world ethics are bound to be involved, including the most honourable way to treat visitors.

I wrote DESIGNING COUNTRIES as an icebreaker to facilitate people meeting each other. Unlike most other inter-cultural visits, I made it a rule that visitors must always be made welcome, as can be seen from the last sentence of Participants' Notes. The aim was to achieve an icebreaker, not an icemaker. In any case, in almost all countries throughout history there has been a tradition of hospitality to the stranger at the gate. One problem with inter-cultural simulations that have no such rule, or which are not carefully briefed, is that some participants tend to (a) assume that the facilitator (teacher, instructor) wants a simulation of racial or cultural conflict or (b) think it would be fun 'For our group to make it hot for the others'. Here are the two main documents taken from the simulation. (See K Jones, *Icebreakers. A Sourcebook of Games, Exercises and Simulations.*)

DESIGNING COUNTRIES   Facilitator's notes

DESIGNING COUNTRIES is a simulation in which the participants work in groups to design their own countries and welcome visitors.

Numbers
Probably the minimum number is six. There is no maximum.

Time
Allow about two or three minutes for each participant.

Materials
One or two copies for each country of the **Notice of Laws**, **Advice to Visitors** and **Impression**. Facilities might include soft drinks. Beware of having armchairs as they have a tendency to block channels. Photocopying facilities could be used for circulating the Advice to Visitors forms after being filled in by the countries but before the visits take place.

Procedure
Hand out the **Participants' Notes**, one copy for each participant, but retrieve all the copies before the event begins. Divide the participants at random into groups. With six there could be three groups of two, with sixty there might be ten groups of six. Hand out the Notice of Laws, the Advice to Visitors and Impression. Set a time limit for designing the countries, otherwise visitors from other countries could find themselves turned away or ignored.

Debriefing
Most countries will already be known to the participants, so the debriefing could start with the wastepaper basket – the rejected ideas. The process of design is usually more interesting than the final result. Avoid getting into the 'Our country is best' argument and be wary of emotional and personal criticisms ('You were just a dictator'). The simulation was an icebreaker, not a personality test.

DESIGNING COUNTRIES   Participants' notes

DESIGNING COUNTRIES is a simulation in which the participants work in groups to design their own countries and welcome visitors.

The **Notice of Laws** is for you to write down any unusual laws. The **Advice to Visitors** sheet is to record any sort of information that might be useful – climate, ways of life, etc. You keep **Impression** in the visitors' departure lounge so that they can sign their names and add their comments, if any, as they leave.

Do not take too long designing your country – the general picture, plus one or two details, is all that is required, and you can polish up the image as the visitors arrive and depart. Take it in turn to visit all the other countries. Officials of the host country and the visitors should introduce themselves.

The *only* firm rule about designing the countries is that visitors must always be welcome.

The simulation HUMAN ZOO comes from my book *Imaginative Events* and is set sometime in the future. I did not classify it as an icebreaker since the format is based on separate group discussions followed by a general meeting of all participants. This is distinct from the format in DESIGNING COUNTRIES and also DETECTIVE STORY (see Appendix) which create a more fluid series of meetings. The skills envisaged are those of communication, diplomacy and planning within the context of race. The activities in the book are classified under three headings: creativity areas, efficiency areas and personal areas. HUMAN ZOO is included in the section dealing with personal areas.

Personal areas embrace the thoughts about oneself and others as human beings, as distinct from human resources. It includes one's own ethics, attitudes, beliefs, emotions, artistry, sympathy, competitiveness, selfishness, compassion, understanding.

The situation is that people from another race are making demands of the Earthlings. Each of the five areas has its own working paper about the pros and cons of setting up a human zoo on that territory and each has a copy of the message from the space explorers. This is purely an Earthling simulation; there is no role for the aliens.

The briefing sheet and the message are as follows.

HUMAN ZOO   Briefing

This is a simulation set in the future in which rulers of Africa, America, Asia, Europe and the Middle East are faced with the problem of Space explorers who have arrived with the object of studying the main life form and requested a human zoo to enable them to do this without causing general disruption to life on Earth.

You will first meet in your geographical groups. You will have the text of the message from the Space explorers plus a working paper drawn up by your own regional advisers. Then you come together for a joint summit conference.

Do not play act. Behave professionally.

Greetings Earthlings

We are the crew of the spaceship Explorer. We study the main life forms of planets. We are here to study beings that are human.

We wish not to disrupt life on Earth. We, the Explorers, are radioactive and our physical appearance is highly repugnant to humans. We propose that you provide us with a human zoo. The zoo is not to exhibit different races, but to show different human behaviour in work and in play, in private life and in public life. We wish to study all typical human behaviour, except war.

The zoo must contain protective shields, observation panels and study areas. It must be at least six square miles in area. It must be operational within six weeks. Inhabitants of the zoo must not leave until we have completed our study.

We wish to know immediately:

- in which part of the world the zoo will be located
- who will inhabit it
- how the inhabitants will be chosen
- what behaviour will be included.

We should, with the greatest regret, consider any refusal or any delay as a hostile act and would, forthwith, order our Security arm to use whatever minimum force may be necessary to achieve our study objectives at a place of our own choosing and in a manner of our own choosing.

Chapter 3

Design

CREATIVITY

There is a story about a sculptor who had just finished making a stone elephant. He was asked, 'How did you do it?' He replied, 'I chipped away those bits that did not look like an elephant.'

Simulation design can be rather like this. Most people think of creative work as building, but it might be just as useful to think of it as chipping away. The simulation designer starts with a thousand potential simulations and ends up with one.

Creation involves closing options. Should the simulation be closed or open-ended? Should it be on a national or a local level? Should there be group roles or individual profiles? As each of these questions is decided, a great many possible simulations have been chipped away.

When a teacher inspects a package of simulation material, he or she may think that the author started off with a nice clear objective and the simulation was arrived at by some sort of logical deduction. What the teacher does not see is the author's wastepaper basket.

Authors must speak for themselves on this question, but I have not met one who regards creative writing as a simple matter of moving from a starting point, which is an objective, to a conclusion, which is the finished product, rather like a motorist plotting his journey on a map. Creative thought processes seem particularly difficult to recall afterwards – it is not like remembering what one bought at the supermarket. It involves a great deal of appraisal, discarding, selecting, and altering, and sometimes changing things around completely because of some new idea.

It is difficult to describe what is meant by design in a simulation. Some simulations have style, elegance, wit, and are not unnecessarily complex. A small number have a touch of genius, bringing a gasp of admiration for their ingenuity or profundity. A well-designed simulation has balance, the parts fit together well, and there is sometimes a degree of ambiguity, allowing different assessments of its meaning and impact. With simulation writing, authorship is not usually enough; there has to be a testing of the product. Unlike writing a novel or a poem, the author cannot simply submit it to a publisher or ask for an expert opinion – it has to be tried out – and it is unusual for a simulation to be right first time. Often it needs considerable alteration and re-testing.

So what advice can be given to someone who wants to design their own simulations? A cursory glance at the academic literature on simulation design will reveal a wide variety of step-by-step recommendations, usually in the form of a flow diagram of sequential steps, something on the lines of:

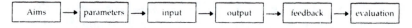

This seemingly plausible guide is about as useful to designers of simulations as it is to designers of clothes or ocean liners. It is not just that empty labels are strung together, but that they are sequential and therefore restricting. Why should aims be completed before input is considered? Although feedback can occur only after something has been produced, why should not the results affect the declared aims, or affect the parameters, input and output? In an effort to meet this objection some academics introduce a series of backward and forward pointing arrows, looking rather like the diagram of a railway network. However, a new objection emerges. As the arrows increase in number the diagram loses its flow and its sequence, and is little better than a vague checklist of individual tasks.

Even as a checklist it misses the point. Authorship is not about a series of tasks, it is about imagination, values, consistency and so forth. Some authors suggest that without a sequential flow diagram or a checklist of tasks there would be no guidance at all, leaving authors at the mercy of aberrant inspiration. This is a misconception. One can be systematic without being sequential. As mentioned in *Designing Your Own Simulations* (Jones, 1985) there are four basic questions:

1. What is the problem? – issue, situation
2. Who are the participants? – roles, identities, powers
3. What do they have to do? – job, decision-making, function
4. What do they do it with? – documents, materials, instructions, existing knowledge.

These are not steps. Nor need an author ask and answer the questions explicitly – since all completed simulations contain implicit answers to these four questions – otherwise it is not a simulation. If the questions are asked as a conscious part of an author's methodology, then they can be asked in any order, at any time during the creative processes, and can be asked and answered more than once.

CONSISTENCY, BALANCE AND PLAUSIBILITY

These three concepts are basic criteria for judging any simulation. Is the simulation consistent within itself? Is it balanced or does it have part-time or passive roles? Is the scenario plausible? The three concepts tend to merge together on occasions: what is implausible may be inconsistent, and what is inconsistent may result in a lack of balance in the simulation.

A useful starting point is the question: 'Within a particular situation is such-and-such plausible? This is not the same question as 'Does the situation imitate real life?' Simulations, in the sense used in this book, are not imitations. Nor need they be simplifications of real life, nor are they real life itself. There is room for analogies, metaphors, and upside-down 'reality' to see what happens when situations and positions are reversed. Plausibility does not require roles to be human. There could be roles for raindrops, ants, aliens, robots and gods. In DETECTIVE STORY (see Appendix) the participants are ideas in the head of a detective story writer suffering from writer's block.

61

Plausibility is a concept which can prevent imbalance. For example, in most, or all, simulations the participants can be warned not to invent key facts and that any peripheral facts they invent should be plausible. Some large-scale situations, military, political, social, or cultural, have a plausibility control, one or more persons with the job of authorizing plausible 'facts'. Otherwise the 'facts' remain as they are in real life – unsubstantiated allegations and the inventor's reputation can be damaged. For example, if a participant tries to gain an advantage by inventing favourable 'facts', such as 'We make the best widgets, our widgets have won prizes', the other participants can say, 'Where is your evidence for that? Show us the document that says so. You are just inventing stories.'

Consistency tends to be undermined by author-muddle. An author writes a simulation, tests it out, 'improves' it and offers it for publication on the assumption that the final version will work well. But changes to one part may have imbalanced other parts, or made them less plausible. The final version may arrive on the desk of the facilitator untested, despite claims that 'the simulation has been tested'. Thus, it may contain contradictions which catch the participants unawares, making it necessary for them to step out of role to deal with the inconsistency. Inconsistencies may encourage some of the participants to become actors, players, students, or gods. Some key facts may be omitted or contained in the wrong role cards. Most notes for facilitators say little about possible danger areas, presumably because the authors are unaware of them or assume that examples of what went wrong are always caused by a few participants and are untypical.

Examples of inconsistency, imbalance and implausibility

Play acting

A role card in a simulation might say: 'Your role is boss and you are angry about shoddy work.' This invites the play acting of anger and removes from the participant the full authority of function, an essential part of a simulation. The facilitator might be appalled by this turn of events and in the debriefing ask the boss whether the sackings were in the best interests of the company. The reply might be: 'No, I knew it was bad for my company, but I sacked half the staff because I had to show how angry I was. I was play acting anger. That is what I thought I had to do. That is what my role card said'.

Funny-name role cards

It is a common fault of simulation design to give 'funny' names for roles. A simulation with the format of a committee meeting involves Chinese Communists in 1927, planning their revolution, including its military aspects. There is a role for a Kuomintang spy, whose main aim is to wreck the revolution by adversely influencing the committee's decisions. Yet everyone has a silly name: Comrades Pong Ping, Chieu Kud, Ho Hum, Yu Too, No Wei and Mee Pee. The jokey names are completely at variance with the detailed historical facts which are contained in the role cards. The names positively invite the participants to lurch into jokes: 'Now then Pong Ping, what ideas can you bat across the table?' or 'Are you objecting again, No Wei?' The stage is set for a slide into 'fun'. Surprisingly, the author of this simulation is aware of the problems and in the Facilitator's Notes he refers to:

> the danger of playacting, adopting comic foreign accents and impersonating stereotypes. Such an approach runs the risk of trivializing the whole thing and reducing it to a vulgar brawl – not to mention a racist caricature. Not many people have the flair and theatrical skill needed to carry it off with the combination of naturalness, wit and conviction that it demands.

As in life generally, awareness of a trap is not in itself sufficient to prevent one falling into it.

Balance

If an objective is to enhance communication skills, then the introduction of part-time or passive roles will unbalance the event. Usually this is an author's mistake. If it was deliberate it would be deliberate imbalance, for example a simulation involving a group that is employed and has tasks to perform and another group that is unemployed and has no jobs to do. However, such deliberate imbalance is often temporary and the idle hands soon find something to do – mischief, sabotage, playing games, protesting, walking out, inventing their own business company, etc. Similarly, balance does not exclude unfairness if unfairness is the aim. In STARPOWER, some participants are rich and others poor, but this unfairness is not imbalance. Everyone participates. It is a mistake to assume that, when the Squares are given authority to change the rules, the Triangles and Circles are standing around twiddling their thumbs. On the contrary, those excluded from decision-making are likely to be very active indeed, discussing, planning, executing, or walking out of the event.

Usually, lack of balance is not only undesirable, it is unnecessary. A typically imbalanced simulation is to have roles for citizens and roles for helpful agencies, but without any provision that all the agencies should be visited. What happens is that the non-visited agencies become bemused, bored, apathetic or turn into saboteurs. Filling in questionnaires afterwards, they mark the 'did-not-like' box. It is not uncommon for authors to conclude: 'There is always a small minority of participants who do not like simulations'.

Imbalanced 'facts'

A common fault is to have role cards with inconsistent information. One simulation has roles representing the local authorities in six towns which have concert halls which might be suitable for a tour by a musical group. The role card for the representative of Barreberg says that the Albertville concert hall has very poor sound quality but the Albertville representative is given no such information. This fault can lead to stepping outside the simulation and appealing to the facilitator.

> Barreberg: Your hall has very poor sound quality.
> Albertville: Who says so?
> Barreberg: It says so on my bit of paper.
> Albertville: Well, your bit of paper has got it wrong, our hall has excellent sound quality.
> Barreberg: (stepping out of role and appealing to the facilitator) Is my bit of information correct?

Alternatively, the participants could remain within the simulation and invent 'facts' to support their case.

Barreberg: Your hall has very poor sound quality.
Albertville: No it hasn't. We have very good sound quality
             and our dressing rooms are excellent.
Barreberg: They are not better than ours and we provide
             free drinks for the groups.
Albertville: We pay our groups far more than you do – and
             we have pretty girls.

Another design fault is that Albertville's role card is the only one that mentions payments, an elaborate and implausible set of rewards in which the town where the group stops first receives 30 per cent of the gate receipts, and the second town receives only 5 per cent, and so on. Does Albertville step out of role and establish the figures as official, or conceal or distort this information? The facilitator's notes do not mention these inconsistencies.

Lurching into chaos

If a simulation does not supply the key facts to the appropriate participants, it is either a badly designed simulation or not a simulation at all; perhaps role play in which the participants are authors or gods. Or more likely, it will be an ambivalent in which some participants are treating it seriously while others invent humorous 'facts' or 'facts' designed to 'win'. For example, badly run international affairs simulations tend to suffer from what is referred to as the 'Armageddon Syndrome' with countries vying with each other by creating fictional violence until everyone is dead.

We have just sunk your battleship.
No you haven't, we have built a tunnel and our soldiers have
captured your government and you are our prisoners.
No you haven't, we captured your soldiers and our air force
has just bombed your country and you are all dead.

The event is no longer a foreign affairs simulation, it is anarchy. In some respects it is similar to STARPOWER because it involves a shift of roles and power. But whereas STARPOWER grants legislative power to one group and does so explicitly, in the above example the facilitator has inadvertently allowed anyone and everyone to seize scenario power. The facilitator has allowed them to abandon their role of politicians and take on the role of gods creating their own worlds – magicians, authors, power-crazed inventors. Plausibility is a point that should be spelt out in the briefing – it rarely is.

Another way in which a simulation can lurch into anarchy and chaos is to distribute power unequally. For example, a foreign-affairs simulation, involving large and small powers, may marginalize a team from a small country. Who wants to talk to it if it has nothing to offer? This imbalance can create disaffection, apathy or sabotage. If it is necessary to have a team without much power, then the designer should make provision for unemployment. Unemployed (bored, dismayed, resentful) teams should be given an alternative role: 'You now represent World Television' (The United Nations, The leader of the Peacekeeping Force) and here is your role card.'

An ill-balanced problem

An indoor version of a supposed out-of-door management training simulation has four teams searching for treasure. The team who gets the treasure home in the quickest time is the winner. A briefing sheet tells the participants that there are five hidden keys, but only one will open the treasure chest. The Trainer's Guide says 'A top team will consist of team members who can put a wide range of management skills into action', and lists 11 such skills. The participants are told that the aim is to give practice in the skills of leadership, communication, problem-solving, decision-making, time management, teamwork, and so on. The participants and facilitator are led to believe that the team that brings back the treasure quickest is the team with the best skills. The inconsistency is that luck is involved. It is impossible to work out (a) which key will open the chest, and (b) how many keys are required to get to the chest safely. So the team getting the treasure back first may be aided by luck not management skills, in which case the debriefing could be hot to handle, a possibility not mentioned in the Trainer's Guide. The inconsistency could easily have been avoided if the problem had required all five keys to open the chest or if it had been possible to work out which key would fit the lock.

Other common inconsistencies include inappropriate mechanisms – for example, it is appropriate for a simulation about fishing to use a dice to determine the weather but not in a parliamentary simulation to determine the outcome of the vote.

Gender and race

Balanced gender is often neglected. In one simulation, there are six roles for members of a golf club, all have masculine names. It is best to avoid first names, if possible, or to use ambiguous ones – Pat, Sam, and so on. Another simulation has role cards in which the cleaner is female and the boss is male. The role card of the boss says:

> A member of staff, Joan Wayne, has been late three times this week. Her uniform is also dirty. Your Assistant Manager, Tom Green, is taking work home; he seems under pressure. It is your wife's birthday tomorrow.

Racial stereotyping is another imbalance between seriousness of purpose and a play acting result. As mentioned earlier, the original version of STARPOWER staggered into play acting, with the 'blacks' leaping on tables and demanding their rights.

Another well-known simulation about a run-down tenement has race and gender faults. The role card of the landlord contains a portrait of him, white, male, a thin moustache and pointed nose. He looks somewhat smug and sinister. In the background is a large house and a big car. Here is an extract from the card:

> The tenement is not in good condition... You are not particularly concerned about the conditions. There is a housing shortage in the town and you know there will always be people willing to rent the rooms. [One family] are West Indians and you charge them an excessive rent because you know they will find it difficult to find accommodation elsewhere...

This is an open invitation to play acting. The participant, male or female, is being forced to mimic an unfeeling, immoral person. For that participant the event is not a simulation, it is drama. Also, it puts the participant in a most invidious position in the action and the debriefing.

> West Indian family (in debriefing): Why were you so unfeeling and racist? Didn't you care if you got a bad reputation, maybe reported in the media?

Landlord: I was forced to play act a heartless landlord who exploited West Indians.

Not all participants in the role might be able to defend their actions adequately. Hatred of the landlord within the event (on one occasion the participants tried to 'murder' him) might carry over and leave an undesirable residue after the event, despite any explanations in the debriefing. And if the facilitator allows the simulation to run on and there is no debriefing, the potential for personal damage increases since the landlord will have no opportunity to defend him or herself.

ETHICS

Two different kinds of ethics can be involved in simulations:

1. the outside ethics relating to what other people do in the real world; and
2. the inside ethics relating to what the participants do during the event.

Each of these two types of ethics can be explicit or implicit. Each type can be inherent in the materials or introduced by the participants or by the facilitator.

There are plenty of simulations related to outside ethics – simulations about drug abuse, poverty, the environment. These issues will almost certainly be covered by the facilitator's notes and the activities are probably run because the facilitator has selected the event because of the ethical issues.

This chapter will concentrate on the second type, ethics within the event, the values, feelings, and beliefs which arise in the minds of the participants during the action and which are sometimes implicit in their behaviour. This is an area of immediacy, it exists in the event, and it is part of the responsibility of the facilitator to avoid unnecessary damage to the participants and to elucidate and explain, particularly if deceit is present.

Petranek (1994) says that at conferences on simulation there is often open acceptance of necessary deception and that probably this position was established because some facilitators dealt with participants only once or never realized the long-term effects of 'a little deception'. Petranek reports that he ran a course consisting entirely of ten simulations in which it was clearly explained that participation was voluntary and that ethical issues were discussed.

> However, over the weeks of interaction in this course, students expressed their anger and hurt from being deceived even a little bit. In some cases, it took me the rest of the semester to win back the trust from some students ... Do not deceive the participants.

This is a somewhat extreme position and would rule out STAR-POWER and some other excellent simulations. But it is good to see more concern these days to protect participants from unnecessary or unjustified hurt. Research workers, in particular, are very concerned about deception:

> There are ... two frequently mentioned dangers of deception experiments, to which some experiments are more liable than others. First, some critics have voiced their concern that lying to people may lead them to lose faith in their fellow human beings. Because scientists are ordinarily highly respected, the discovery that a scientist will lie might upset subjects even more than lies told by others. Secondly, and perhaps more importantly, it has been pointed out that some deception manipulations are emotionally disturbing to a subject, and the disturbances might not be entirely amenable by debriefing.
> (Walster, Berscheid, Abrahams and Aronson 1967)

As pointed out by Stewart (1992), there has been little discussion of ethical considerations in experiential learning compared with considerable discussion by research workers in the field of experiments. She urges facilitators who use games and simulations for experiential learning to focus on ethics in their debriefings if the event involves deceit.

> For example, if a simulation-game encourages participants to lie, the debriefer must be prepared to discuss the morality of lying and its negative effect on both the liar and the person being lied to.

She goes on to say: 'It is unethical to conduct an experience-based activity without providing an adequate debriefing'.

However, even if we accept Stewart's recommendations there are practical difficulties for the facilitator.

- Ambivalents do not normally come with a health warning on the package. Rarely does an author say: 'Deceit is involved'. Discrepancies between the 'facts' given on role cards, which can involve deceit, are rarely mentioned. The notes for simulations which have 'hidden agendas' often fail to advise the facilitator to use the debriefing to reveal what is hidden.

- Facilitators' notes rarely mention personal ethics involving the participants and tend to concentrate on 'outside ethics'. Authors tend to regard their simulations as satisfactory if they achieve their objectives, for example, making people more aware of housing needs. They usually neglect to mention psychological hazards implicit in the event. The facilitator can be caught unawares. 'There was nothing in the materials or my briefing which made them behave like that' is a common response to emotional outbursts and distress.

- The area of concern is wider than deception by the author/ facilitator. Even without any element of deception, a simulation can result in psychological damage, such as hurt feelings, anxiety, and stress.

- In the case of an ambivalent, the facilitator is ill-equipped to deal with any psychological damage. Had the facilitator been aware of the likelihood of incompatible methodologies then presumably the event would not have been used or the briefing would have explained the nature of the behaviour required – 'This is a game and you have a duty to try to win'.

- If the facilitator's concern about ethics is related only to 'outside ethics' (people should not be too greedy in society, etc) then damage can be intensified if participants feel that general criticisms are directed at them personally. This could be worse than having no ethical discussion at all.

- The accusations of dishonourable conduct may come not from the facilitator but from the participants themselves, either during the action or in the debriefing. In the case of an ambivalent, no one, particularly the facilitator, is likely to have the necessary methodological concepts to defuse the situation. Attempts to pacify and mollify could succeed in damping down flames, but leaving a dangerous, smouldering resentment.

● Even if the facilitator is aware of the deceit, or of the clash of methodologies, and merely announces this fact in the debriefing, this may not in itself be enough to expunge the feelings of distress and hurt. As Tesch (1977) points out, the hidden assumption is that the debriefing will create a magical undoing, 'an eraser for emotional and behavioural residues'.

Here is an example, based on personal recollection, of a simulation with potential emotional and behavioural residues. Pairs of participants took roles to discuss moral and social problems relating to college students. Two role cards were on the following lines:

JOHN

You are a moral tutor at the College and you will be interviewing Nora, who has been a student at the college for one year. Recently, her mother visited you to say that she was very concerned that Nora may be taking drugs. She had noticed that Nora's behaviour had changed and that she seemed to mix with the 'wrong crowd' and may be sleeping around with boys.

NORA

You have been a student at the College for one year and will be interviewed by John, your moral tutor. You feel that your work has been fairly good. Your chemistry results have been below average but you are now making a real attempt to tackle the subject and your teachers think you will make progress. You have an attractive personality and have no difficulty making friends.

Nora's role card invites play acting, as personality is stated. Also, some participants might object to taking the role of the opposite sex or feel inadequate in such a role. However, the main problem is John 's role card. It is inadequate in 'facts' and morally dangerous.

The obvious question for John to have asked the mother was 'Have you discussed this with your daughter?' The participant receiving this role card probably assumes that the accusations have substance, otherwise the simulation should have been the meeting between John and the mother, not the interview with Nora which could go like this.

John: It's good to see you. How are you liking college?
Nora: It's all right. I think I am getting on all right.
John: What about your social life?
Nora: It's all right. I'm making friends.
John: I must ask you this – what about drugs?
Nora: Oh no, I never take drugs.
John: And sex? Do you wish to discuss that?
Nora: No problems there. I concentrate on work.
John: We are concerned about your welfare.
Nora: Yes.
John: Would you like to add anything? Anything about drugs or sex?
Nora: What do you mean? Are you accusing me of lying?
John: Oh no, not at all. But I should tell you that I had a visit from your mother.
Nora: *What?*
John: I don't necessarily believe this, Nora, but your mother said she thought you were into drugs and were sleeping around with boys.

At this point, the interview could take various courses.

Emotional

The participant, female or male, in the role of Nora storms out of the event, humiliated and distraught at the thought that her hypothetical mother had gone behind her back and falsely accused her. Her impression is that John had virtually accused her of lying. She sees him as an obnoxious, sanctimonious, prying hypocrite, and vows never to speak to him again, even though she knows the event is not 'real'. The person, male or female, in the role of John is also likely to be distraught and may well feel humiliated and confused by the outcome. If Nora does not leave the role card behind her for John to read, then feelings of guilt and resentment are probable.

Bewildered

Nora realizes that John's cards must contain the information about the 'mother' and John realizes that Nora's card cannot have mentioned drugs or sex. Both start to invent 'facts' to keep the simulation going. Nora confirms or denies the allegations and John tries to think of 'facts' which could give plausibility to the interview with the 'mother' and justify the invasion of Nora's privacy.

Professional

Both participants realize they are in a badly designed simulation and stop the event. They show each other their role cards. They discuss what they should do next. Should they play act, change roles, treat it like a case study, invent more 'facts', or complain to the facilitator?

Whatever course is taken, it will be difficult for either participant to forget the incident, particularly the participant in the role of Nora. The two people might find it difficult to sit together in future. If, during the event, there is no emotional explosion and if it is not raised in the debriefing, the other participants and the facilitator may be unaware that anything untoward has occurred.

Competitive

One aspect of ethics that is frequently misunderstood is the question of competition in an event. Some trainers, and rather more teachers, believe that in competitive activities the pupils, students, and trainees are learning the wrong thing and are being indoctrinated into a materialistic and selfish type of behaviour in which material possessions and winning is all. Basically, there seem to be two criticisms: the duty to try to win has priority value, and this is undesirable and/or the scoring mechanism is entirely materialistic, for example, no marks for ethics.

Here are three opinions about competitive 'events'. As we have noted, the words 'game' and 'simulation' tend to be used inter-changeably.

1. Such games can and do create tensions, show-downs and often fierce competition. That these factors produce a state of adrenalin flow is not surprising. That this extreme attitude can always be useful is questionable (Ravensdale, 1978).
2. Games of skill have the possible educational disadvantages of discouraging slow learners, dramatizing student inequalities, and feeding the conceit of the skilful (Abt, 1968).
3. If a simulation were designed to include such constraints ... [concern for the environment, etc] it would be a 'bad' training experience, for participants would be trained in methods of thinking and setting decision priorities which would put them at a disadvantage when it was time for them to compete in the real world. However, it would be foolish to condemn the class of business simulations for this significant lack; they are doing their job, which is training (Zuckerman and Horn, 1973).

Here again, it is useful to look at the concepts. Is the criticism related only to games? If this is the case, then all games are guilty since all games, as distinct from puzzles, problems, and exercises, are necessarily competitive. Real-world ethics cannot apply, otherwise it would not be a game but a simulation or role play. If teams representing companies are told that their only aim must be to make the most profit, then not only are real-life ethics excluded but real-life consideration of consequences is also excluded. Despite what Zuckerman and Horn say, companies do have reputations to think about, and executives are human beings with human feelings and they do consider consequences, whether they act ethically or not. In any case, to criticize a game because it involves competition is an error of category. A game is a game, take it or leave it.

By contrast, simulations do not incorporate scoring systems that are not part of a plausible environment. Otherwise, they are games, or exercises, or ambivalents. If the word 'winning' is correctly applied to a simulation, for example, a court-room simulation, the 'scoring' is not made by dice or the turn of card or an accumulation of bonus points. The decision is made by judge or jury and this is entirely proper and entirely ethical – it is part of the system of justice. In any case, 'winning' is an end-term. It ignores what actually happens, the preparation, the communication skills, the arguments, and the substance of the case. It also ignores possible real-life consequences, the judgement might be overturned on appeal.

In simulations involving committees (groups, forums, mass meetings, or parliaments), 'winning' is a legitimate word in phrases such as 'winning the argument' or 'winning the vote'. But this 'winning' may have nothing to do with materialistic values, nor with a desire to 'win'. The winning argument may favour altruism, kindness, or charity. The 'winner' may have no selfish desires whatsoever and be motivated entirely by a desire to right wrongs.

To sum up:

1. The ethical problems of teachers and trainers regarding competition in simulations can be illusory. The real issue may be a misunderstanding of methodology and terminology.
2. Similarly, misunderstandings of methodology and terminology may blind authors and facilitators to very real psychological damage in simulations or, more usually, in ambivalents.
3. Any simulation involving any kind of deception or potential emotional disturbances should be very carefully debriefed with plenty of opportunities for participants to get things off their chests.

ICEBREAKERS

Simulations that are intended to be icebreakers come into a special category that determines when they should be used, namely when ice has formed. The metaphor of icebreaking is apt. An icebreaker is a vessel designed to clear a passage in frozen waters and open up channels of communication. In human terms, icebreakers are intended to deal with frosty situations, cold starts, or nervous freezing. They aim not only to break ice, but also to warm the atmosphere. A 'warm-up' is another name for an icebreaker. By contrast, the social mixing and introductions in everyday life are very hit and miss. They can be difficult: one can forget names, not know what to say, and if embarrassment turns into panic then the mind can go completely blank or one can burble like an idiot. An icebreaker helps to overcome such problems.

Icebreakers tend to be misunderstood. They need not be limited to activities at the beginning of courses. They can be used whenever ice has frozen communication. If, halfway through a course (conference, convention, workshop), the trainees (students, conference-goers) have formed themselves into cliques based on sex, race, jobs, or any other criteria, then an icebreaker could be well worthwhile.

Another important consideration is that icebreakers can do other things as well. For example, they can develop skills, create talking points, encourage empathy, or illustrate situations in the real world. Thus, they could be used irrespective of their ice-breaking properties if they meet the needs of a course or session. The label 'icebreaker' should not deter trainers and teachers from using the events in other situations where they would be effective. In addition, icebreakers need not require the participants to break ice, merely to have the roles and functions which require them to meet other participants to fulfil a task. Perhaps the major consideration is the amount of interaction implicit in the event. Thus, team simulations do not necessarily make good icebreakers as participants may have little contact with members of other teams and this may, indeed, serve to create ice.

Ice can also be created by invading privacy or causing embarrassment. A simulation (or is it play acting?) in which participants are required to go about emitting the noise of animals in order to find 'mates' could be counter-productive. Unfortunately, many published icebreakers (games, exercises, simulations) tend to be childish and suitable only for party entertainment or for behavioural therapy. This is not because there is anything wrong with party games, psychotherapy, or drama sessions. They are all very useful and respectable techniques. But for the purposes of teachers and trainers, it may not be a good idea to include personality probes or intrusive questions if the intention is to break ice. Also, most serious icebreakers tend to be dull, offering little challenge to the intellect or the imagination. Usually they are perfunctory exercises of the getting-to-know-you type, where the participants move around for 20 minutes and ask each other about their hobbies.

There are various objectives which might be involved:

1. match names to faces;
2. get to know each other on an intellectual, problem-solving level;
3. find out how imaginative and/or humorous people are;
4. meet on the level of organizational efficiency, or inefficiency;
5. discover people's aptitudes in creative authorship;
6. seek personal friendships and warmth;
7. have formal contacts;
8. talk formally to colleagues and make short speeches;
9. reveal attitudes, views, beliefs, likes and dislikes;
10. display skills of journalism and presentation; and
11. exhibit ability to analyse situations and problems.

Social factors might also be considered. Do you want the participants to hurry around meeting each other? If so, it is probably better to pick a game rather than an exercise or simulation, since the desire to win will increase speed of movement. Similarly, if the normal social behaviour of the participants is keenly competitive – which in practice seems to mean that most of them are males – then that is a reason for choosing games, or avoiding games, depending on your general attitude.

Most people can cope fairly easily with routine situations but are less efficient when something unusual occurs. So if you want to encourage flexibility of mind, look for the unusual, the imaginative and the creative. Here are a few categories:

1. imaginative, routine;
2. open-ended, one right answer;
3. real-world, fantasy;
4. subject (business, social, political, economic, scientific); and
5. personal.

The question of timing is somewhat different in icebreakers from other interactive learning events. Since the aim is to meet people, it is convenient to give an approximate time, related to the number of participants. Meetings, if only for one minute each, take time. The times given in the Facilitator's Notes are dependent on how many people you want the participants to meet, all of them, most of them, or about half of them?

For a detailed example I include DETECTIVE STORY in the Appendix taken from my book *Icebreakers: A Sourcebook of Games, Exercises and Simulations.* This simulation is unusual because of the roles, but it is a simulation, it is an icebreaker, it is complete and it can be photocopied and used within the institution that purchases this book.

DETECTIVE STORY can be classified as imaginative, open-ended and an opportunity to get to know people on an imaginative level as distinct from the sort of icebreakers which merely involve an exchange personal information or involve a routine task. The mechanics are designed to cater for large numbers as well as small. For example, if two participants meet and find they have the same role card, they merge and stick together as the same 'thought'.

Some authorities on interactive events in general advocate having a debriefing which lasts at least twice as long as the event itself. My own view is that, with icebreakers, a debriefing of five to ten minutes should be sufficient in most cases, unless the event has been brought into the course for reasons other than its icebreaking properties – communication or social skills – in which case a longer debriefing could be contemplated.

Chapter 4

Choosing simulations

PROBLEMS

One of the main problems in choosing a simulation is that neither the reading of the facilitator's notes nor an inspection of the documents can reveal the flow of interaction which occurs during the event. Viewing a simulation from the outside is not like reading a poem. The best part of the simulation – the action – is missing. Some of the most interesting and imaginative simulations contain all sorts of clues, suggestions and options which are deliberately buried at various levels, and these finer points of design are rarely mentioned in the facilitator's notes.

If it were merely a case of difficulty of evaluation it would not be too bad. One could then accept the lack of data, and be open minded. Unfortunately, teachers and trainers who have little if any experience of simulations almost inevitably jump to a conclusion which is unfavourable. Looking at the materials from the outside puts them off. If there are a lot of documents, despite the fact that most of them may be read only by one or two participants, the simulation is judged as being too complicated. If, on the other hand, there are only one or two documents then the event looks empty and the reaction is that the participants would not know what they were supposed to do.

Even teachers who are experienced in running simulations often have difficulty in guessing how well a particular simulation would work in practice. There is no real substitute for participation.

However, if the facilitator's notes inform the teacher that the event requires a couple of hours to run, then it is unlikely that a full participatory trial would be possible. The usual advice is that a teacher should read the documents and then take on a role and imagine the situation as seen by that person. Although this is certainly better than a non-imaginative approach, it still means that the first step is to read all the documents, and this can interfere with the imaginative participation. An easier introduction is to read the notes for participants and step inside the event by taking a role and reading only the documents which that person would have.

FACILITIES CHECKLIST

Before shopping for a simulation it is useful and time-saving to make a mental inventory of the conditions and facilities which will be available. The greater the facilities, the greater will be the area of suitable choice.

Money

Like shopping for anything else, the teacher or trainer is looking for value for money. The educational value of a simulation is not always reflected in the price, or the weight of the documents, or in the length of the list of worthy aims, or the gloss on the package. As with any sort of shopping, the more experienced the buyer the greater the chance of a bargain.

An important financial consideration is whether the publisher has given permission for documents to be photocopied for classroom use. At one time permission was hardly ever given, but in recent years several publishers have made this concession. Permission is usually restricted to the school or college, and usually includes only the documents for participants, not the facilitator's notes.

The books or packages of simulations should make it clear whether photocopying is allowed, and if not whether the materials are durable or whether they will be used up by record keeping and form filling. If the simulations allow photocopy and are in book form, then it is useful to note whether or not the book has a spiral binding. A stiff spine can make photocopying difficult, and there is the possibility that repeated photocopying may cause the pages to come adrift from the spine.

Numbers

Most simulations are extremely flexible in the number of participants that can be accommodated. However, it is useful to check whether the simulation can deal with the number of students in the class. This information should be featured prominently, and should include minimum and maximum figures.

Some facilitator's notes contain options for running the event with numbers that are larger or smaller than the ideal number, but if these options are not spelt out, then the following considerations may help.

In the case of a larger number of participants than roles there is a choice between (a) participants sharing roles, and (b) running the same event simultaneously in different groups.

Sharing roles is usually no problem, but in some cases there is a danger that the resulting group will be too large. For example, a committee simulation with 10 roles could be an unwieldy committee if increased to 20 members, and unless the time allowed for the meeting was also doubled then there would be less time for individual participants to make their contributions.

Simultaneous simulations are easy to arrange – say one group in each corner of the room – but there can be problems of noise interference if the event concerns public speaking rather than informal discussion. On some occasions it is possible to link simulations which are run simultaneously. For example, there could be several appointments boards, but instead of each having their own separate candidates there could be a group of candidates who could individually rotate from one interview to another.

With fewer participants than roles the options are (a) to abandon some roles, and (b) to have one or more participants taking on two roles.

Time

The materials should give an idea of the average amount of time needed and whether this includes the briefing and debriefing.

As with numbers, time is fairly flexible in most simulations. If the time required appears to be too long in an otherwise suitable simulation, it is often possible to reduce the briefing time by a different form of presentation, or reduce the overall time by greater efficiency in the general running of the simulation. Similarly, a short simulation can be lengthened by various means, including a more thorough preparation, and an elaboration of some of the formalities and procedures within the simulation.

It may be a mistake to assume that the less able pupils need more time than brighter pupils to deal with a simulation. They may take more time to read and understand what they are supposed to do, but in the action part the brighter pupils spot more opportunities and will delve, prod, argue and discuss.

Time has a value, but there is a danger, as with money, in assuming that the less spent the better. Some authors argue the opposite. Elgood (1976) writes:

> Time is not at all a bad measure of value, and if certain items of knowledge are thought to be worth a major allocation of time, then the message of their importance tends to get over more strongly.... It is too seldom admitted there is a positive correlation between the thoroughness with which people learn a thing and the effort they expend in doing it. Intellect is only one of the characteristics that is involved in the learning process. There must also be an emotional evaluation of the importance of the knowledge and this tends to relate to the emphasis placed upon it by the circumstances in which it is offered.

Ability

The main difficulty in assessing whether the materials are on the right level for the students' abilities is that these abilities cannot be assessed with any certainty without the students taking part in several simulations first. So if the teacher knows the students' abilities in simulations, all well and good. But if the teacher's views on student abilities are based on what happens in teacher–student orientated learning, the assessment may be inaccurate. Teachers who have had little or no experience of using simulations tend to underestimate the ability of their students to cope with the materials – not so much in the first simulation where there may be teething troubles, but in the subsequent ones. Even during the course of the first simulation it is often possible for the facilitator to notice the gradual (and sometimes not so gradual) increase in skill and confidence of the participants in handling the situation in which they find themselves.

The problem becomes somewhat easier if the simulations are graded. This technique is becoming increasingly popular, with simulations linked together like steps, the early simulations being relatively easy and the others progressively more difficult. Sometimes simulations are graded within themselves, with preliminary exercises, trial runs, or simplified versions of the main simulation activity.

Another consideration is the possibility that individual students who have low ability or a limited knowledge of the language might be thrust into an embarrassingly prominent position. Role allocation is dealt with in the next chapter, but generally speaking simulations involve group work and work in pairs. This provides opportunities for shelter.

Unlike the normal classroom situation, individuals in simulations are less at risk of personal exposure. To be asked a question by another participant is less fraught than if the questioner is the teacher. Moreover, in simulations the questioning is not on a personal level but on a role level, and this is an important distinction. The duties inherent in roles usually embolden the low achievers and the shy.

Materials

Some simulations require additional materials. These can range from paper and pencils to computers. They are usually listed in the facilitator's notes and are the sort of items which are readily available. However, there are often other materials which are not listed but which can be added to increase the realism or add to the effectiveness of different aspects of the simulation – a vase of flowers, an in-tray, a ten-minute break in the canteen for coffee, large sheets of card and felt-tipped pens. This point is dealt with more fully in the next chapter.

Room space

Room space is important in those simulations where several groups are operating simultaneously, particularly if it is desirable that they should meet in privacy (or secrecy). International affairs simulations and competitive business simulations are cases in point where an additional room or two can remove all temptations to observe or spy on what the other groups are doing.

However, if the simulation is right for the participants but only one room is available, then it is still possible to manipulate the geography of the furniture so as to lessen the chances of espionage.

OBJECTIVES

Just as authors sometimes design simulations, then find out what they have created and add the objectives on afterwards to fit the likely achievements, teachers might like to consider doing something similar.

This suggestion may sound like educational heresy, but it does have certain practical advantages for the teacher.

First, it means that the teacher's assessments and objectives are firmly based on observation – on seeing what actually happens. This is important in simulations, since what happens is often unexpected and may pass unobserved if the teacher is firmly concentrating on some predetermined objective.

Secondly, it is an attitude of mind which can broaden the spectrum of objectives. Instead of sticking to the obvious, it may encourage the teacher to look for other objectives as well and to evaluate all sorts of incidentals, which may seem peripheral but could be important, particularly to the participants involved.

Thirdly, it reduces the danger that the teacher will be conned by a high-sounding list of objectives contained in the publicity material for the simulation. Simulations have to work well to be effective, and objectives are not achievements. A good simulation with no objectives attached is preferable to a poor simulation with thousand well-meaning aims.

Fourthly, the sort of additional objectives that are likely to arise from actual observation of what is going on in a simulation are probably those associated with the abilities and skills which make up so much of adult life that are not easy to recognize and may be impossible to quantify. But that does not mean they are not important. Confidence, for example, is tremendously important – so are organizational skills, the ability to use language and communicate effectively, and all sorts of personal traits and attitudes which help people to get on with one another.

In a simulation, important changes in a person's thinking and behaviour can occur and yet pass unnoticed because the teacher is concentrating on whether, for example, the participants are appreciating the problems involved in the use of land resources.

The argument is not that objectives are unimportant, rather the reverse. Objectives are so important they should be constantly appraised in the light of observation and experience. If a teacher finds that a particular simulation is consistently successful in achieving some unexpected yet desirable learning behaviour, this can be added to the list of objectives. If expected attainments do not occur, these can be dropped from the objectives. However, apart from choosing a suitable simulation and presenting it effectively, there is nothing the teacher can do to ensure that the objectives are achieved; that depends on the participants and whether the objectives are appropriate.

It can be useful, therefore, to examine some of the objectives which authors have listed as important, and see how these may influence a teacher's choice of simulations.

Facts

Many situations, perhaps most simulations, are aimed solely at conveying facts and insights about a particular subject. Some of these are training simulations, designed to familiarize the participants with the subject and the procedures for dealing with it.

Some are tailor-made simulations for a specific company or organization and are intended to give the trainees a feeling of what it is like to be doing a specific job. These, however, tend to be guided exercises rather than genuine simulations, and in any case there is little question of choice involved as they are often so specialized as to allow no adequate substitute. Factual simulations are easy to justify in the classroom and staffroom, as they are likely to be directly relevant to forthcoming examinations.

But of all the objectives which a teacher may have, the conveyance of facts about a specific subject is the most limiting as far as making a choice is concerned. If the teacher wishes to introduce a simulation about a specific event or historical development – the Wars of the Roses, for example, or the growth of railways in Africa – there may be few if any simulations to choose from. As there is now a rapidly growing number of simulations being published, however, it is worthwhile for teachers to delve into directories of simulations and publishers' lists to see what is currently available. As with any other form of learning materials, it is up to the teacher and trainer to assess the quality of the facts provided – their accuracy, their significance, their presentation – in the usual way. The teacher must exercise professional judgement and take into account the reputation of the author and publishers.

If the facts are contemporary, not historical, the teacher faces an additional problem – the facts may be (or may become) out of date. This is particularly the case in simulations which deal with the specific and current social services, agencies, benefits, laws and regulations. Since such simulations convey an important feeling of immediacy and relevance in the areas of personal issues and general problems, students may well conclude that this is how things actually are in the details about pensions, job security and housing. The teacher can look at the publication date and try to update the materials or can explain that certain facts are no longer true; alternatively it can be presented as an historical simulation.

Choosing a simulation for its facts is not the same as choosing a textbook for its facts. In a textbook, the facts are there to be learnt; in a simulation, the facts are there to be used. If in a simulation the participants decide that some of the facts are irrelevant to what they are trying to do, they may dismiss these facts with no more than a quick glance. If the simulation has a huge scenario, with page after page of background facts which have little relevance to the action, not only may the facts go unlearned, but a feeling of annoyance may arise which has a negative effect on fact learning.

If, on the other hand, most of the facts presented in the simulation are potential weapons in a conflict of interests, they are likely to be scrutinized far more closely than would ever occur in reading a textbook. As well as learning relevant facts, the participant would be developing valuable skills of selection, analysis and presentation.

Models

In simulation literature the word model does not imply miniaturization, in which all the details are reproduced but on a small scale. When talking about simulation, the word model is used to cover the essential working elements of something – an economy, a political system, a society.

If the teacher's objective is a model, the choice is far wider than if the objective is to convey specific facts, because models do not have to be based on actual facts. Sometimes fiction and fantasy can provide a clearer picture of the way things work than an attempted simplification using actual organizations and specific examples. Fiction can be manipulated by the author to highlight essential aspects in a way which may be difficult to achieve with actual real-world components with a lot of historical and perhaps irrelevant clutter.

There is no right answer to the question of whether to choose simulations with actual names, organizations and places, or whether to choose simulations using fictitious elements. The familiar has the advantage of being easily identifiable; the unfamiliar has the advantage of giving the students an opportunity to take a fresh look at an old problem.

A model based on fiction may have to go into detail about procedures and background simulation 'facts' which might be unnecessary if actual organizations were used. On the other hand, a model based on actual names and places may run into the problem of which 'facts' are real, and can bias the outcome of the simulation in favour of those students who happen to know the most about that specific organization, country, or period.

Decision-making

Decision-making covers a wide variety of skills and disciplines. It is not the same as decision-giving; it is not just saying 'yes' or 'no'. Making decisions involves searching around for the most suitable decision, analysing the situation, and constructing hypotheses about what might follow certain decisions.

One of the problems of training is that people are trained to solve the same sort of problems and make the same sort of decisions again and again. This is why many courses in business management deliberately seek out unusual problems in order to broaden horizons and shake up established thought patterns.

So, in having decision-making as an objective in choosing simulations, the key question is the sort of decisions that are required. Are they specific, or are they general? Should the decisions be unfamiliar in order to give students practice in coping with the unfamiliar, or should they be restricted to previous decision-making experiences?

An advantage of unfamiliar decision-making is that it changes the existing classroom hierarchy which is usually dependent on factual knowledge. With new problems students have more equality of opportunity.

The same consideration applies to open and closed simulations. In arithmetical-based business simulations, the arithmetic is an objective criterion for measuring the success of the decision-making. The problem is to crack the code and this is done by analysing the result of round-by-round decisions.

In closed simulations there may be one right answer or several, but there is an objective criterion which enables students to say 'Oh, yes, I see, we got it right (wrong).' Open-ended simulations, on the other hand, may not only lack any objective criteria, but may also be deliberately designed to provide simulation 'facts' of equal weight to conflicting interests to balance arguments and make everything a matter of opinion. Behavioural and human relations simulations tend to be open-ended; so do conflict simulations in local government or international affairs. In open-ended simulations the decision-making is not a neat and tidy scientific affair.

However, in a simulation, unlike an examination, the result is rarely important. What matters is how the result is arrived at. Secondary school pupils tend to prefer closed simulation because they satisfy a 'What's the answer?' approach to learning. Whether this is a good enough reason for a secondary school teacher to select closed simulations is another matter. The teacher may take the view that one objective is to try to persuade the pupils out of the habit of asking, 'What's the answer?' to anything and everything. In many areas of life 'What's the answer?' is not an appropriate question. Questions themselves can be more important than answers. Exploration can be preferable to arrival. Decision-making can concern opinion as well as fact.

Communication skills

Through effective communication, we deliver our ideas. It is useful to be able to communicate and even better to be able to communicate effectively. It is inefficient for brilliant ideas to be concealed by inarticulate mumbling.

One of the great advantages of simulations is that they are self-activating and provide scope for a far wider range of useful communications than normally occurs in education. Instead of the student communicating with the teacher, usually answering questions to demonstrate that something has been learned, in a simulation the student learns *by* communicating.

It is also useful to remember that emotions and motives can be important elements. In simulations communication is motivated by feelings and beliefs – about poverty, power, life, love.

Simulations in the same subject field can often cover a wide range of communication skills – diplomacy, arguing, interviewing, reporting, note taking, drafting, editing, organizing, presenting a case, speaking in public, listening. In many schools pupils go in at one end and come out at the other without any personal contact with many of these skills. Practice brings skills, and skills bring confidence; without practice there is no confidence. Many students hate the idea of speaking in public and would run a mile if asked to take the chair or to present a case. Yet these skills have a wide transferability. The skill of diplomacy is of value to all people, not just diplomats. The ability and confidence to speak in public are of value to others who are not public speakers. Being able to speak in public does not mean that one has to do so; but it can be most satisfying to know that one could cope if the occasion arose. Obversely, lack of practice, lack of skills and lack of confidence can on occasion result in near mental paralysis if a person is afraid of being called on to speak.

If practice in communication skills is one of the objectives of the teacher in choosing simulations, it is probably a good idea to seek out simple, argumentative and emotional simulations as starters. Some simulations are specifically designed to encourage communication skills and all simulations involve communication. So it may be worthwhile looking at the difficult part of a simulation – the bit that is left out – to see what sort of communication is involved. If there is a series of simulations on the same subject, this could be a gradual way of giving communication practice. Alternatively it may be better to look for a wider variety of roles and situations to cover more skills.

Fortunately, the specific subject is not all that important since it is difficult to be clear and articulate in one subject without also being good at communicating other subjects too. Preparing one speech helps to prepare the next one, even if the subject is different. Diplomacy in international simulations may help diplomacy in family and personal relations.

Language skills

Language skills are allied to communication skills, and sometimes the two phrases are used interchangeably. In practice, language skills are usually taken to refer to the sort of skills taught by the English department or by teachers of English as a foreign language and these are not identical.

Yet, in both fields, the first problem may be to encourage the students to talk. One teacher in a north London secondary school observing his class take part in their first simulation, said with astonishment, 'I've never heard half of them speak before'.

It is not just a question of language, but a question of confidence. Simulations have the advantage of removing the teacher, who is sometimes an inhibitive figure, respected yet feared. To the shy student it may be better to keep quiet rather than say something wrong and be laughed at.

The British Council is in the forefront of advocates of simulations. Kerr (1977) says:

> They ensure that communication is purposeful (in contrast to the inescapable artificiality of so many traditional exercises and drills); and, secondly, they require an integrative use of

language in which communicating one's meaning takes proper precedence over the mere elements of language learning (grammar and pronunciation).

If language is high on the teacher's list of objectives, subject matter is probably a good deal lower down. It may be a prescription for failure to set out with the aim of matching the students' interests with the subject matter of the simulation. If the teacher has a group of Spanish engineers as students, it is courting disaster to place a blind order for a simulation that is about (a) Spain, (b) engineering, or even (c) Spanish engineering. The scenario may be bulky, the language content may be slight, and the interaction virtually non-existent. The main language skills may come afterwards when the participants complain that 'It is not like that' in their branch of engineering or in their part of Spain.

Behaviour

Quite a number of teachers introduce simulations for exclusively behavioural objectives and these can vary considerably. One is the straightforward objective of improving the behaviour of the class. If there have been antagonisms, frustrations and tension among pupils, boredom or dissatisfaction with the course, or potential hostility between pupils and the teacher, a good simulation can work wonders. It removes boredom, redirects the activity, and extricates the teacher from a confrontation.

Other behavioural objectives can range from self-awareness to an examination of the hidden motives and attitudes in society. By their nature such simulations tend to be controversial on all sorts of levels. For example, Zuckerman (1973) notes that most racial attitude simulations ask the participants to get into the black experience. He says this encourages 'shallow depth responses along the line of "Lo, the poor black man, who is so mistreated by those *other* people" '. Shirts (1970) says that simulations about the black community are generally written by people from the suburbs and are based on a series of unfounded clichés about what it is like to be black, which not only encourages stereotyping but creates an attitude of condescension towards blacks. Also, says Shirts, such simulations can give the students the impression that, having taken part in the simulation experience, they know what it is actually like to be discriminated against or what it is like to be black.

These criticisms are not altogether satisfactory. For example, if there is stereotyping, this suggests that it is not a simulation but an informal drama. If a role card for a member of the housing department says, 'Generally does not favour allocating houses to blacks in white areas', this is personality imprinting – a stereotyping that denies the participant the right to make up his own mind in the light of the situation. Similarly with the question of condescension, unless it is role-play in which the person is asked to behave in a condescending manner, condescension is no more predictable than sympathy or respect. In a genuine simulation, the participants can feel any way they like, providing they do their job as best they can.

Behavioural simulations, like textbooks or television programmes, may or may not be typical of specific problems. But no medium exists in isolation and any individual example in any medium is unlikely to convince a student worth his salt that he 'knows it'.

In addition to the 'big issues' there are plenty of what might be called 'local' behavioural simulations. Interview simulations are a case in point. The objective is to help the participants behave more effectively in interviews.

There are personal conflict behavioural simulations – conflicts between boss and employee, between parent and child, between teacher and pupil. Some of these are close to role-play exercises, but others are genuine simulations involving groups of people, documents and decision-making. The dividing line is not so much the number of participants or the documentation, but whether it is teacher-guided, whether it is personality-imprinted, or whether it is based on job function.

Friendship

Friendships develop in simulations and there is no reason why they should not be added to a list of objectives. Indeed, some teachers use a simulation for no other purpose than to help students get to know each other at the beginning of the academic year. Not only does it help students get to know each other, it also helps the teacher to get to know the students in a way which is different from restrictive teacher–student orientated behaviour. With simulations it is quite common for episodes to occur which take the teacher by surprise. 'I had no idea that Mandy had it in her' is a common remark. Consequently, the teacher has learned something, and so probably has Mandy and the other students.

Friendships involve more than just friendly feelings; they imply understanding and communication, and working together effectively. All these can be very useful at the beginning of a course, and pay dividends later on in work which might be completely dissimilar to the subject matter of the simulation. Teachers may tend to undervalue friendships, thinking them personal, not educational, but they are very important in education just as they are in the world outside the classroom.

Prediction

This category of objective has to be mentioned since it is extremely valuable to certain specialists who wish to find out in advance how certain things are likely to work.

Foreign ministries may want to know 'What is likely to happen if we did so and so?' A simulation is the best method of finding out, short of actually doing so and so. A defence ministry may wish to know the most effective strategy for some newly developed weapon – but it cannot start a war to find out. There is no alternative but a simulation. Local authorities may wish to know if their resources for dealing with disaster are likely to be effective. Again, it is a matter of simulating the situation. But prediction is not an objective that the practising teacher need consider. If it were worth considering, then almost certainly the teacher would already be using predictive simulations.

Selecting

The bulk of the work of selection has been done once a teacher has assessed the resources available and has settled on the objectives. All that remains is the practical step of examining and trying out potentially useful simulations.

The additional points to watch for have already been dealt with in earlier chapters – the need to look at the design of the simulation, to see if it is fully participative, if it is well balanced, if it is provocative, stimulating, interesting, emotional, involving, and so on.

If the selection of the simulation is appropriate then the answer to whether the simulation will work effectively depends on the participants and the skills of the facilitator. These issues are dealt with in the next chapter which concentrates on simulations in action.

Chapter 5

Using simulations

PARTICIPATION

If the teacher participated in a simulation at the choosing stage, all well and good. But if not – perhaps because the simulation had already been chosen and was awaiting the teacher's use – the teacher should arrange a participation session with a few friends or colleagues.

Some teachers protest at this advice, because they see it as a waste of time. They see the simulation in the same light as a book or film and think that all that needs to be done by way of preparation is to inspect it. If it is not possible to persuade or bully people into having a complete run-through, at least the teacher should make every effort to enrol a few people for participatory sampling, as suggested in the last chapter.

With something like an arithmetical model-based simulation the teacher should actually fill in a decision form and process it – perhaps with other group decisions – in order to arrive at the resultant number which comes out after the data have been fed through the arithmetical formula.

The sort of thing which can happen is that a group fills in forms wrongly without knowing it and so receives 'wrong' answers as a result. By the time the students have acquired enough experience of the simulation to realize that something is wrong, it may be too late to unscramble the mess. Everyone will have to start again or abandon the project – and either eventuality will do nothing for the teacher's reputation. Reading the instructions and saying 'I don't need to try it, I understand it' are famous last words.

FACILITATOR

Although the participants 'own' a simulation this does not mean that the facilitator's role is unimportant. On the contrary, the facilitator has vital and varied functions, including observing and assessing.

The first job of a novice facilitator is to shake off any inappropriate habits or thoughts derived from the experience of teaching or instructing. The main part of every simulation, the interaction, is not taught. By training and by habit teachers interrupt, guide, explain, give hints, smile, frown, and in many subtle ways (including silence) try to help students learn. But if a teacher tries to do this in a simulation, it stops being a simulation and becomes a pseudo-simulation or a guided exercise.

Even during the briefing and debriefing it is useful if the relationship between facilitator and students is that of the relationship between professionals – respectful, polite, slightly distant but enthusiastic about the speciality – in this case simulations.

Once into the action, the facilitator should aim to be invisible, to merge into the background or to assume the protective colours of a plausible role such as usher, messenger boy, furniture remover, or friend of the editor or managing director. When it becomes necessary to speak to the participants, it is most valuable for the facilitator to adopt appropriate protocol. Instead of saying, 'If any student...' or 'If any participant...', it is better to use the appropriate titles – 'If any Honourable Members...', 'If any executives...', 'If any councillors...', 'If any journalists...'

As mentioned earlier, the concepts of autonomy, consistency and plausibility are vital, and these provide guidelines for the facilitator and for the participants. Reality for the participants is the interaction. It is theirs; they own it. Conversely, what happens (or is supposed to happen) outside the area of the simulation is the responsibility of the facilitator, or the organizing team if it is a big simulation. This means that if any participant orders an event to happen outside the room – calls for a day of prayer, calls for troop mobilization, calls for a strike, calls for a protest march, calls for the police – it is up to the facilitator to decide what happened and to inform the participants accordingly in whatever manner seems appropriate within the realism of the simulation.

Some simulations have their own built-in mechanism which makes this unnecessary. In management simulations, and within specified limits, certain orders are automatically carried out according to the mechanism. Nevertheless, should any group of participants wish to take decisions outside their area which are not covered by the 'rules', it is a matter for the facilitator alone to decide what happens.

The participants have power within the simulation interaction; the facilitator has power outside it. Power, authority, duty and responsibility are thus clearly defined and are clearly separated by the line between inside and outside.

DETACHMENT

Within a good simulation facilitators are often subjected to the strongest temptations to participate themselves. In the swirling action, the vigorous arguments, the emotional, imaginative and momentous events, the facilitator can sometimes be observed grinning with excitement and holding back from rushing in to participate. Extraordinary though it may seem the teacher some-times does actually sweep forward and assume some role or other. This is bad intervention. There can be good intervention if, for example, a key role is obviously vacant. Perhaps there should be someone in the role of Secretary-General of the United Nations for a few moments, or a policeman, or a king, or an usher. These are temporary interventions to assist the mechanics, rather than interventions for personal reasons. It is a general and a safe rule never to interfere, nor to give any signs of pleasure, displeasure, surprise, boredom, annoyance, appreciation or exasperation.

A poker-face is virtually obligatory. It is not easy but is worth cultivating since it deters students from looking at the facilitator for signs of acceptance or rejection. Poker-faces help to preserve participant power and responsibility. At first this may seem strange and unusual to the participants, but they soon see the value of it and take pride in 'owning' their simulation, which would be impossible if they had to keep looking over their shoulders at the facilitator.

This detachment by the facilitator could be explained in the briefing: 'My job is to remain poker-faced. There should be no point in your looking at me. Should you see me smiling or frowning, I am not doing my job properly. Try to take no notice of me at all. A simulation is not like a play; you are not going to be coached and guided and stage managed. We are not aiming for a perfect performance. You are on your own. You've got a job to do. Just do your best and ignore me.'

OBSERVING

With some simulations the facilitator has no problems about observing what is going on without interfering in the action and without disrupting the participation. If the simulation is a public debate, the facilitator can sit poker-faced in a corner of the room and can see and hear just as much as any of the participants. But a problem arises when groups meet separately and in secret. Should the facilitator pull up a chair and say, 'Don't pay any attention to me' and listen to what is being said? With three or four groups, the facilitator could move about and enter the intimacy of the circle of confidential talk, and then move off and on to another group. Is this a good idea? Is it a good idea even if the facilitator resists all temptation to smile, frown, look appreciative, perplexed, or whatever?

In general, the answer must be no, it is not a good idea. If it is a straight choice between ignorance and interference, it is better to remain ignorant rather than risk distraction or interruption or subtle manipulation.

This is because what happens happens, and the interaction should be the sole responsibility of the participants, without interference. It can, of course, be recollected and discussed in detail at the debriefing. The group can say, 'We had a lot of trouble deciding whether to do so and so, and Mr X said such and such and Miss Y replied . . .' The fact that the facilitator did not listen to the actual conversation is not important; what is important is that it took place.

This advice may be very difficult to take. Teachers like to know what is going on. If they know what is going on, they can use the information afterwards and give advice, hints and guidance in the debriefing. It is all part of the teaching technique to observe and comment.

But a simulation is not teaching. It is learning and the learning will be placed in jeopardy by interference. The learning is not just the learning of facts; it is behavioural and concerns power and responsibility and should not be diminished. No teacher walks into a cabinet meeting or boardroom meeting and says, 'Don't mind me, I'm not here, just carry on normally.' If such a remark is to be made, it should be made during the briefing, not in the middle of the action.

There are, however, certain techniques for observing without interfering. One technique is to walk around slowly at an even pace, moving from group to group but avoiding eye contact. Another method is to sit at a 'blind' spot, perhaps in a corner of the room, or take a seat at the side if two groups are facing each other.

ROLE ALLOCATION

Teachers and trainers who are experienced in using informal drama and role-play exercises probably have their own favourite method of allocating roles. But a simulation is quite different from an exercise and an informal drama. Different considerations apply and what may be suitable for the one may be unsuitable for the other.

There are two kinds of roles – group roles and individual roles. These can be considered separately even though there are many simulations which contain both forms.

Group roles

It could be a group of business executives, government ministers, tribespeople, or whatever, but the key question is which group the individual participants should belong to, rather than what their function will be as members of that group.

One question is whether students A, B and C, who always work together, should be allocated to the same group. Another question arises if groups have important distinguishing characteristics which evoke preferences or prejudices. For example, who should belong to the Bosses' Party and who should be members of the Workers' Party? Role allocation can be random or by individual preferences, or by teacher selection. Each has advantages and disadvantages.

Teacher selection has the advantage of putting the decision-making into the hands of the existing classroom authority – the teacher – who should be best placed to make the selection on whatever criteria may appear appropriate. The teacher can keep together a group of friends or can split them up. Deliberate selection allows the teacher to restore the balance of arguments in a simulation by placing the more able students in that group which is the least popular among the students, eg the chemical company management rather than the anti-pollution protesters.

There are potential hazards in teacher selection of group roles. One is that it may arouse resentment among the students; they may feel manipulated or discriminated against. If so, this would be contrary to the basic principle of simulations which is to give as much power and responsibility to the participants as possible.

Another problem is that if the teacher and students are new to simulations, the criterion of student ability may be inappropriate, since it would be based on normal classroom behaviour and results. Surprising things can happen in simulations and the usual hierarchy can be rudely shaken.

Probably the easiest method of allocation to groups is to keep together those students who usually work or play together. This still leaves the problem of bosses or workers, landlords or peasants, hunters or farmers, traditionalists or revolutionaries, but it does mean that during the course of the simulation there is a minimum of friction within individual groups. Naturally, the strength of this arrangement depends on the strength of the group feelings in the class.

The random method of group allocation offers a solution to several problems simultaneously. First, it is fair and can be seen to be fair. It avoids allegations of favouritism. It helps the students to assume the responsibilities and duties of professionals, and it helps to establish the teacher in the neutral roles of facilitator and observer.

The main disadvantage of the random method is the resentment felt by friends who find themselves separated. You could explain, however, that this is one of the hazards of life, and that it is a good idea to try to cooperate with people who may not be friends and may sometimes be enemies. This disadvantage is likely to diminish as students widen their circle of acquaintances and friends, which could turn a short-term disadvantage into a long-term gain.

It is worth making the point that random selection really should be seen to be random and not an announcement, 'I'm randomly allocating student A to the king's party and student B to the slaves' compound.'

Some simulations can be re-run with a change of group roles in which case role favouritism is no longer an issue, and this leaves only the problem of the composition of the teams.

Individual roles

An individual role means that an individual has some particular function, responsibility or knowledge which is different from the other participants.

For the facilitator, a key problem is what to do if a simulation has a role or roles implying specific skills, such as a technical expert. An important consideration is whether the scientific data are available to all the participants, perhaps in a 'library', or are restricted to the role card or documents belonging to the expert. It may also be that the public documents contain only general scientific evidence while the individual role card and private documents give additional evidence in detail.

Other considerations are whether the scientific evidence is disputed. Are there two or more 'expert' views, or does the simulation provide only one undisputed view? How important is the scientific evidence in a given simulation? Are the overriding factors public opinion, financial priorities or statistics about acceptable or unacceptable levels of pollution?

Answers to these questions will help in deciding how to allocate the role of expert. If individual roles are allocated at random and student X or Y or Z gets the role of expert, does that unbalance the simulation or render it less effective? Or are there safeguards? Can other participants unearth the information and question the testimony of the expert? Does it matter much anyway since the educational aim is likely to be practice, not perfection?

Cases should determine decisions. But it is probably a good idea, in those simulations where the role of expert is of some prominence, to allocate the role at random but to allocate two participants to the role. They will back each other up and it is not unrealistic for an expert to have a colleague or assistant. This technique can also be used in simulations which require the role of chairperson, whether in the national assembly or the public inquiry, or a sub-committee of the local boys' club. Even if all the participants are themselves top-level adult experts, it might still be a good idea to consider whether it would be desirable to allocate a second person to a role – perhaps deputy speaker, deputy leader, deputy chairperson, deputy prime minister.

The arguments in favour of randomness in individual role allocation are similar to those already given in the allocation of groups. The technique is fair and is seen to be fair. People can develop by having responsibility, and the aim is to give opportunities, not to engineer perfection. Random allocation enhances the principle of participant power, and at the same time it strengthens the role of the facilitator by emphasizing the facilitator's impartiality, thus avoiding the damaging accusation of role manipulation. As with group allocations, the main disadvantage of randomness in individual allocations is likely to be in disrupting the pattern of friendships or working acquaintances. But this is likely to be temporary and may well have longer-term benefits. The most difficult simulation for random role selection is always likely to be the first simulation; afterwards it becomes much easier.

An alternative to random choice and teacher selection is to allow the students to volunteer for specific roles. In practice, this is not usually a good idea because of possible disputes or feelings of unfairness. It opens the door to the extroverts to seize the best (or easiest) roles. Resentment about this may seethe beneath the surface and can damage the effective running of the event.

PRESENTATION OF MATERIALS

What should be a simple matter of presenting the right materials at the right time seems to cause far more trouble than it should. Possibly one explanation is that the teacher has not participated in the event and fails to appreciate the importance of sorting out the documents before venturing into the classroom – perhaps using colour coding, envelopes, paper clips. It may help, for example, to have the notes for participants photocopied on non-white paper.

The need for care in presenting the materials is not simply because it is more efficient to do it properly. Another reason is that in a simulation the penalties for mistakes are likely to be greater than in traditional teacher–student situations. If, in normal classroom discussion, the facilitator has to fumble around to find the right bits of paper, this may be rather annoying or amusing to the students, and they probably do not object to the delay. But in a simulation, which tends to develop a considerable dynamic quality of its own with a great deal of involvement, any delay caused by facilitator inefficiency may well result in considerable exasperation from the participants. Furthermore, the mechanical breakdown may jerk the participants out of their roles, and it may take them some time to re-establish the flow and realism of the simulation.

The actual loss of a document can unbalance the simulation to such an extent as to make it virtually unworkable. In ordinary classroom teaching, the loss of one fact-sheet out of ten may not be disastrous, but in a simulation, where the pieces fit together and are often interdependent, the loss of one part can easily nullify the whole. So the facilitator must allow sufficient time to see that all the required documents are available and that they are arranged in the right order for presentation.

In preparing and arranging the documents, the facilitator should consider not only the action part of the simulation, but also the briefing. Are any additional documents desirable in order to clarify the basics of the simulation? For example, if there are no notes for participants, it may be a good idea to prepare some – perhaps half a dozen sentences outlining the main points. Not only will this inform the participants, it will also offer a safeguard in case the facilitator omits some vital information in the verbal briefing. It avoids the facilitator being placed in the embarrassing position of having to interrupt the simulation and say, 'Sorry, I forgot to tell you that . . .'

If the facilitator does not prepare or present any notes for participants, it is useful, possibly essential, to prepare a checklist of points to make during the briefing. Various home-made documents can also help to explain to the students how the mechanics of the simulation will operate. The facilitator might draw up a chart or diagram or map showing time sequences, location of furniture, and so on.

Other types of materials and equipment can help to make the simulation more efficient or more plausible, depending on the situation. Here are a few examples: clean note pads and sharpened pencils, little flags, name tags, labels for locations, word processors, typewriters, telephones, pocket calculators, vase of flowers, clock, coffee and biscuits, wastepaper baskets, formal message pads, tape recorder, video camera (for media simulation), clip boards, maps, tray of paper clips, carafe and glasses of water.

CLASSROOM FURNITURE

The question of the geography of the classroom furniture does need to be thought out beforehand. Provided the teacher has already participated in the simulation, there are no real problems about where to put the tables and chairs, but plenty of opportunities to add to the realism.

The starting point can only be the simulation itself – its nature and structure. The requirements can be one single table around which everyone sits or separate tables or areas for different teams or individuals.

If secrecy is important, teams should be as far apart as possible – perhaps one in each corner of the room, or with separate rooms of their own, as recommended in some business and foreign affairs simulations.

Some simulations change the pattern of interrelations at different stages, and in this case it is important that the classroom furniture should be changed as well. It may seem a chore to move a few tables around, but it is always useful and sometimes essential that this should be done.

A team should have a base from which to work. This should be allocated by the facilitator to a suitable spot, bearing in mind the location of other team areas, the facilitator's own area, and the likely traffic between bases.

Should the simulation involve interviews, furniture arrangements should copy the normal furniture arrangements for interviews. In a public inquiry the chairperson and advisers should have one table dominating the room with the other chairs either facing this table in rows or as cross benches if there are 'for' and 'against' parties.

What should not happen is that the teacher walks into a class in which there are neat rows of desks, simply hands out material and asks the students to form teams and find tables for themselves. This is a prescription for time-wasting and muddle. If some teams should be close to each other, the facilitator must arrange this; if far apart, this also should be indicated. Maps of the classroom showing which groups sit where at each stage of the simulation can be useful. Such classroom plans not only save time but allow the students to do their own furniture moving.

If the simulation involves a map of a geographical area on which countries (teams) are represented, the classroom geography might be copied from the map, with neighbouring countries having neighbouring teams. This may cause an espionage problem if the neighbours are hostile. There are several ways of solving this: a screen between the two teams, a strong warning against 'cheating', espionage not being allowed, or the two teams sitting facing away from each other.

The location of the facilitator's desk should be within easy access of all the participants, but preferably not impeding busy traffic routes.

If the facilitator has to fumble uncertainly with classroom furniture during the course of the simulation, this is almost as bad as not getting the materials right. The facilitator who says, 'Well, perhaps we might put this desk here, and you could go over there – you, not you – and then we'll have those materials over here on this table' can disturb the concentration of participants who are in the middle of an exciting and involving experience.

Special provision will have to be made if the simulation includes the media – newspaper, radio or television. Each media organization should have its own base with the necessary equipment.

A studio can be a problem for teachers and trainers who are not experienced in this sort of thing. However, a simple and acceptable solution is a tape recorder with a microphone placed on a chair on a table. A coat over the back of the chair placed between the microphone and any likely source of external noise helps to improve the quality of the recording.

Broadcasts should always be live. (Fancy recorded inserts rarely work and take away the personal quality of immediacy.) They should also be done standing up, moving towards and away from the microphone at appropriate moments if more than two people are involved. The alternative of sitting at a table usually introduces a mass of clunks and squeaks as the microphone is pulled in front of the speaker, or chairs are thrust back and forth.

Television broadcasts are much the same as radio broadcasts, except that the viewers should all be at one side of the room and there should be markers to indicate the left and right of the screen to indicate when a speaker moves into or out of camera shot. So all-pervasive is television that this convention is readily accepted by the students. No cameras or technicians are needed.

However, a warning note should be sounded about using available electronics. Many a simulation has been brought to a shuddering halt by failure to operate the equipment correctly. Incidents causing laughter can easily arise through failure to spool tape successfully, cue participants, or edit the videotape. The simulation can grind to an embarrassing halt, rather like a lecture where no-one knows how to operate the projector.

If done successfully, of course, there is the advantage of an electronic record of what happened which can be used for demonstration purposes later. But the facilitator should think carefully before embarking on the use of electronics. Is it necessary? Is it desirable? Is it merely a gimmick? Is it worth risking the value of the simulation? Will the actual process of recording the action detract from the realism? With a news conference, of course, it is permissible to accept that it will be recorded and that things could go wrong in setting up the lighting, microphones, and cameras. But if it is a confidential cabinet meeting, or an interview of an applicant for the headship of a school, a battery of electronics – and the possibility of hold-ups and failure – may not be worth the effort, and would almost certainly detract from the realism and inhibit the action.

Business and military simulations can be different. If these need computers to work out results, they must be provided.

TIMING

The timing of simulations can present problems or involve guesswork as some activities can be completed quicker than expected or continue longer than expected. Again, the teacher's own participatory experience in the simulation is invaluable, not only in assessing how long things will take, but also in drawing up contingency plans in case the timing does not work out.

However, nothing really disastrous can go wrong, provided that no vital activity is started without sufficient time to complete it. If the climax of the simulation is a radio transmission, it will be a shambles if the lunch bell goes when the broadcast is only half completed. Similarly, if a person is to make a set speech, it should not be begun if it cannot reasonably be finished in the time available.

If the simulation contains an activity which has to be treated as a whole and not interrupted, then the timing must be tailored accordingly. Deadlines must be firmly laid down, guillotine procedures established and starting times observed. Deadlines, in particular, must be regarded as sacred. The participants have the role of professionals and they must behave like professionals. If the broadcast is due to start at 2 pm, the participants cannot appeal to the facilitator to 'Give us a few more minutes, we are not quite ready'.

Breaks in simulation activity should not be regarded as necessarily undesirable. They give the participants time to think out their strategies and explore their options. A chat over a cup of coffee or an evening at home can help the participant ease into the role.

In deciding how to fit the simulation into the time available, consideration should be given to the breaks. It is helpful if the briefing, and perhaps the handing out of some materials or roles, takes place on the day before the action, although contingency planning may be needed in case someone does not turn up or unbriefed students arrive.

Some simulations last for days, weeks or even months. In these cases it is sensible to make sure that teams have adequate resources to carry on in the case of unavoidable absences.

STAGES

A simulation which has various stages may present problems in moving smoothly from one stage to the next.

With model-based business simulations each stage may be similar in form to the last one and no great changes need occur. Nevertheless, it is worth considering what should happen when one team finishes its decision-making much earlier than the rest. Do they analyse the data further, do some other task, chat, do crossword puzzles, go for coffee, or snoop on the other teams? The facilitator should have some suggestions to put forward in the briefing, and this means thinking about the problem beforehand. If there is a delay in processing the decision-making forms in order to present the results to the teams, it is useful to warn the participants in the briefing, thus avoiding or reducing any unnecessary frustrations during the action. However, there are various devices for reducing or even abolishing such delays. One technique is to time the end of a session to coincide with a normal classroom break – leaving the facilitator (or clerk) to feed the decisions into the arithmetical model and produce the results in time for the students' return.

Although some business-type simulations still require the facilitator to work out the arithmetic, the advent of pocket calculators has reduced the delays, and if the simulation is computer-assisted then delays are virtually abolished. In those simulations in which the stages are not based on statistical models a break may nevertheless be valuable. Suppose, for example, a simulation includes events which have to be reported in written form, as when political simulations include newspaper journalism. In such cases it could be useful to end the news conference shortly before a break and for the journalists to start writing their news stories immediately after the break. The break allows them time to think how they will present their stories.

Another alternative, which happens in real journalism, is for any long event (conference, debate, public inquiry) to be reported by a team of two or three journalists who take it in turns to take notes and then write their stories.

COMPUTER-ASSISTED SIMULATIONS

As mentioned in the last section, computers can greatly assist model-type simulations by rapidly producing statistics which show the result of decisions made by the participants, or which represent changes in the simulated environment – the weather, the number of hospital beds available, the height of floodwater.

If a computer program is an inherent feature of a simulation then the important issues arising from this will doubtless be covered by the facilitator's notes. This leaves the question of whether computers should be used when they are not a built-in feature, and the answer depends on circumstances and aims.

If there is sufficient time and computer expertise, then the facilitator and/or students can produce their own programs for a simulation which can be of the number-crunching variety, or a data bank. If the aim is to model local housing regulations, or unemployment benefits, or list community services, then such a program could be written, and once written it would be relatively easy to increase the information and update it when necessary.

Equally appropriate would be the use of computers as word processors in simulations involving journalism or authorship. If the software includes facilities for printing large letters and various graphics, then these can enhance the production within a simulation of a page of a newspaper, an official announcement, a company's logo, an advertisement.

Perhaps the main danger of a computer-assisted simulation is that it could reduce human interaction. If one participant operates the keyboard and takes decisions without proper consultation then the other participants would be reduced to passenger status.

Instead of talk and thought there could be silence and dissatisfaction.

Another disadvantage is that some computer operations take more time than is justified by the results, and may be inappropriate, implausible, and inefficient.

Despite these dangers it is certainly worth looking at the options and seeing whether computers can be used effectively.

However, this is saying no more than the general piece of advice – when preparing to run simulations it is valuable to explore the possibilities and potentialities of any appropriate equipment, materials and facilities. These could include typewriters, video cameras, tape recorders, large sheets of coloured paper, overhead projectors, dictionaries, pocket calculators, the help of the art department or the school secretary, the help of an outside expert, magazines, bottle tops, scrap paper, name tags, clip boards, elastic bands.

RERUNS

The possibility of a rerun should be considered before the briefing because it might affect the way the simulation is presented, and also the way the simulation operates. For example, if the students know that there will be, or may be, a rerun, they will have an additional motive for paying attention to what the other participants do, as they themselves may have that role in the rerun.

Reruns allow the participants to switch roles and find out what it is like being on the other side of the table or the other side of the argument. They enable the participants to have another go. This is important, as students are usually self-critical of their behaviour in simulations, and are often far from satisfied with their actions. Knowing more about the simulation at the end than they did at the beginning, they are often anxious to try it again.

For the facilitator, the scheduling of a rerun means that there need be no anxiety that certain 'lessons' or opportunities are missed first time through.

However, no simulation should be rerun unless there is a good reason for it. Simulations which have repetitive stages are unlikely candidates for a rerun, unless the arithmetical model or some fundamental condition is changed. Simulations with hidden agendas are unworkable the second time, because the 'answer' was revealed the first time. Equally unsuitable are simulations which are like puzzles with one right answer.

ADAPTING

Many teachers and trainers adapt materials. Making adjustments to suit the classroom conditions is permissible, but it should never be wholesale adaptation and no part of the author's work should ever be copied or reproduced without permission as this is illegal, being an infringement of the copyright laws. In music, for example, taking a few bars of an essential melody may constitute an infringement of copyright. As far as the adaptation of simulations is concerned, the main danger is that the teacher will start the adaptation before the simulation has even been tried out.

Because simulations are so difficult to assess in their packages, it is often the case that the teacher decides that a certain document is too complicated or that a role is unnecessary, or that a lot of extra facts have to be fed in before the participants can start. The teacher can ruin an excellent simulation in this way. Key bits which are parts of the checks and balances can be removed or rendered ineffective. For example, the simulation may contain a boring, jargon-filled document about health hazards or unemployment benefits, and the teacher may decide not to hand it out. Yet the simulation within itself may generate a need to tackle such a document for some specific purpose – to report on it, to interview someone about it, to use it in an argument as evidence, to ask for its amendment, etc. In the action part of simulations, documents are rarely read dispassionately.

Generally speaking, the teachers who are experienced in using simulations are more willing than inexperienced teachers to run a simulation according to the recommendations of the author – at least for the first run through. This means that any subsequent adaptations will then be based on experience, not guesswork.

For example, what can be done if the simulation works reasonably well but has a bulky scenario which has to be digested before the action starts? There are several possibilities. The information might be fed into the simulation in stages. Some of it might be incorporated into the individual role cards. The mode of presentation can be varied – a letter in students' pigeon-holes, a tape recording, even a telephone call. If the facilitator sifts through the information, some of it might be separated into a 'library' where it can be delved into and skimmed through according to the various strategies and interests of the individual participants.

Should the simulation seem to stick at particular points, with no-one showing initiative, the facilitator can see if it needs a drop of oil – perhaps the introduction of the role of journalist, or of some provocative document.

Similarly, the simulation may seem to be less effective than it might be because of part-time or passive roles. For instance, can a jury be dispensed with? Is it necessary to have a United Nations Secretary-General – or could the facilitator take on this role on odd occasions? Is a banker an essential role or could it be left to the participants to manage their own transactions?

Practice and experience are necessary for distinguishing useful waiting from boring or frustrating waiting. A person waiting to appear before an appointments board may be sitting around and, to all appearances, doing nothing. Yet mentally the participant may be very active in rehearsing strategies and predicting likely questions. Waiting can be alert, watchful and strategic, with the potentiality for action, and the mental recording of who is doing what and why. This is not the same as looking blankly out of the window, reading a comic, doing a crossword, or telling funny stories.

There can be several reasons for adding to a simulation. The addition of 'public opinion' – perhaps journalists – to a foreign affairs simulation can add more realism, introduce a constraint to the use of power by leaders, and provide an impetus to diplomatic moves. The facilitator can add facts – perhaps in the form of leaflets in a 'library' – in order to give more background data and ammunition for argument. If the main aim is practice in communication skills, it might be possible to add a sequence involving a news conference, public meeting, or parliamentary debate.

However, adaptation of this sort should not be undertaken without a good deal of thought and a reasonable amount of experience with simulations. Really major adaptations should not be attempted: it is better to buy a more suitable simulation.

A special case for adaptation is in the teaching of English as a foreign language. But even here, the teacher should give the simulation an unadapted run first, as it is easy to underestimate the ability and motivation of students involved in a simulation.

BRIEFING

Briefing is easy, providing it is based on personal participation by the teacher and on careful preparation.

If the students are unused to taking part in simulations, it is useful to spend some time explaining what they are and what they are not. The key points to emphasize are the extent of the powers, duties and responsibilities of the participants, and also the dividing line between reality within the simulation and the fictional background outside. Even if the students have taken part in simulations before, it is advisable to make sure they are aware of these points.

With careful preparation, the facilitator will enter the briefing well primed with explanatory notes, diagrams, maps, timetables, deadlines, or whatever else is necessary.

If the simulation is simple, the facilitator may be the only person in charge. But with a longer or more complicated simulation it is advisable to have an assistant or even an 'organizing team'. Some teachers who are familiar with simulations prefer giving one or two of the students the opportunity to be facilitator as it gives them practice in organization.

Naturally, the briefing should contain no hints or nudges about policy decisions. Therefore, for the facilitator, the briefing is a very practical session – a checklist of items to be dealt with, points to be made and queries answered. Should the simulation have several stages, parts of the briefing can be left until later and the information given immediately before the stage in which it is needed. The more thorough the briefing, the less the likelihood of unexpected events arising which could interrupt the simulation or knock it off course.

The facilitator should be cautious about giving too much information to the participants during the briefing. A student who is placed in the management team of Blogsville Ropes Ltd might ask, 'Does it manufacture all types of ropes?' If the answers to the questions are available in the documents, it is probably best for the facilitator to decline to answer. In most simulations, it is one of the functions of the participants to find out the facts. If the briefing opens the door to this sort of factual question, other participants can start asking similar questions and the facilitator can end up by spoonfeeding information to the students. Also, the factual information provided by the facilitator in this off-the-cuff manner could be distorted or misleading. It is better to let the students find it out for themselves from the documents.

This will, of course, leave some students dissatisfied and feeling that they do not know enough about the situation. But the facilitator can explain that adequate information will be provided when they receive the materials and that the briefing is concerned with the mechanics of the simulation only.

ACTION

Facilitating some simulations is as easy as rolling a ball down a gentle slope. Even with more complicated or lengthy simulations, it is simple providing the simulation has been well prepared and briefed. The reason for this is that the action tends to look after itself. It has its own power, its own catalysts and its own initiatives. The problem with a good simulation is not to get it moving but to get it to stop.

In a simulation the facilitator is generally in a good position to observe participant behaviour, including fact-learning, strategies, decision-making, problem-solving, and the use of language and communication skills – to say nothing of enjoyment. The facilitator should have a notebook handy to jot down various points as they occur – possibly for use during the debriefing.

The vital task for the facilitator during the action is to make absolutely sure that the right materials are available as and when they are required. Once the simulation is under way, the facilitator should check the materials, which might have been shown to the students during the briefing, and make sure they are in the right order and grouping for handing out or for availability. In some simulations this is unnecessary as all the materials are given to the participants at the start, but any simulation which involves feeding in materials from time to time requires close monitoring by the facilitator.

In addition to the question of materials, the facilitator should also prepare in advance for changes in classroom furniture, timetables or role changes which might be part of the structure of the simulation. With a short simulation – lasting, say, less than an hour – no intervention by the facilitator should be required, assuming, of course, that it has been adequately prepared and briefed. But with longer simulations some minor adjustments in the machinery might become desirable or necessary and, very occasionally, a major change is required. In these circumstances, the problem for the facilitator is whether or not to intervene and, if so, how and when. Effective intervention may require skill, experience and imagination.

When intervening, the facilitator should have two objectives – to interfere as little as possible with the smooth running of the simulation and to select a cover story which fits in with the simulation itself.

Suppose that during a simulation involving interviews or a public inquiry, the facilitator notices that the members of the board or panel say, 'Now then, Mr ... er ... er'. This may indicate either that the person interviewed does not have a clearly written name tag, or the member of the board has no list of names, or both. At the next suitable break the facilitator, adopting the guise of messenger, usher or whatever, provides the necessary name identification material to whoever requires it – perhaps even apologizing and saying that the town clerk's department was responsible for the omission.

With a medium-length simulation, lasting half a day or a day, or a longer simulation which goes on for more than a day, the chances increase of the need for a change in roles. A student may go sick, or may not turn up, thus creating a serious problem. If the simulation consists of teams, the missing member may not make much difference; but if the missing person happens to be the prime minister possessing secret information, it will probably be necessary to halt the simulation in order to make suitable adjustments. Very occasionally a change of role is necessary because of an internal coup. The prime minister may be overthrown because there was a basic conflict between his 'sell-out' policy and that of public opinion as represented by his country's media. The organizing team may have decided that the prime minister was wrong and should be deposed, or 'forced to resign', or whatever is plausible. Any major change of this nature cannot be dealt with peremptorily. There will almost certainly have to be a break in the simulation until the roles are changed, someone else becomes prime minister and the ex-prime minister takes another role.

A role change would be required in a local affairs simulation if the chairman of the council finished up on the wrong end of a vote of confidence because of repeatedly favouring one group. In this case, the intervention by the facilitator might be quite unnecessary, since the participants could deal with the role change within the confines of the action itself – there being no need to hypothesize a general election or military takeover in order to move a person from one chair to another.

It is rarely the case that the unexpected arises unexpectedly. There are usually warning signals and the facilitator should watch out for them. In this way, drastic intervention can often be avoided by taking minor remedial action. Even if a major disruption occurs the facilitator will have had time to work out some contingency plans.

Suppose the facilitator notices that a participant has nothing to do and is looking bored. The question is whether this is slight and temporary or whether something has to be done about it. If something has to be done, it should be within the plausible parameters of the simulation. A note can be handed to the participant from the local council, the editor, the managing director, the shop steward, or the prime minister, asking the participant to help X or Y.

Should any serious misbehaviour occur, probably the best thing is for the facilitator to send the person concerned a note asking the participant to come and take a telephone call, or come and see the cabinet secretary, military commander, etc. Having extracted the trouble-maker the facilitator can find out what is the matter. It might have nothing to do with the simulation, or it might be a misunderstanding, or a failure of the simulation to allow the participant a full role. Having found out what is the cause of the trouble, the facilitator can take whatever action seems appropriate.

It is much easier for the facilitator to deal with behavioural problems within a simulation than in normal classroom teaching since there is no escalation of personal antagonism between student and teacher. The facilitator, by the nature of the job, is not eyeball to eyeball with the students and consequently is a detached and impartial authority.

The main danger in the action part of a simulation is not mis-behaviour so much as inappropriate behaviour, and this may be caused by the failure of the facilitator to explain clearly enough what can and cannot be done in a simulation. As has been emphasized earlier, the participants must be told to accept their function: they are businesspeople, town councillors, or world leaders, not magicians, gods or saboteurs.

Supposing, for example, in a history simulation a Saxon king announces that he has moved his army 100 miles overnight. What happens next? If the simulation has been well briefed, then one or more of the other participants will challenge the decision. One challenge would be to point to some of the docu-ments or to common sense and say that 100 miles is an impos-sible distance to cover in such conditions in such a short time. But a more important challenge would be to say that an order is only an order, and a decision is only a decision, and that the 'facts' outside the room depend on the facilitator. Even if it was an order for an overnight journey of only one mile, it would still be up to the facilitator to decide whether the order was carried out, whether it was effective, and what other consequences resulted from the order. Assume, however, that the briefing was somewhat inadequate, or that the other participants were not sharp enough to realize that the Saxon king had turned into a Saxon magician, what should the facilitator do about the inap-propriate behaviour?

One way is to stop the simulation and explain to everybody that this sort of thing is not allowed; but this has the disadvantage of disrupting the flow of the simulation. Another way is for the facilitator to send a written message to the Saxon king saying, 'My lord king, your army is foraging for food. It is not possible to march until tomorrow.' This should hold the situation until the next break, during which the facilitator can explain the difference between inside decisions and outside facts.

In ordinary teaching it is customary and efficacious for the instructor to step in to correct mistakes of fact. It is also usual to go further than this and offer advice and information about non-factual matters – questions of ethics, values and opinions. For a teacher, these interventions become second nature and habitual. During a simulation there may be an intensely strong and perhaps overwhelming desire to step in, interrupt the action, and convey the correct information or the useful piece of advice. The intellectual justification for this sort of intervention is that if wrong information goes uncorrected it may be learned and reinforced by repetition, and that the facilitator should provide the correct facts in order that they may be put to practical use, tried out, tested and learned while participatory interest is high.

Some authors go further than this. They argue that the facilitator should ensure that the discussion is relevant, that each person has a fair opportunity to contribute, and that valuable points are discussed in plenary session during the action rather than just within one group.

The trouble with this sort of intervention is that it will kill a simulation stone dead, leaving only an instructor-controlled exercise. There is nothing wrong with instructor-controlled exercises, but they should be advertised as such, not presented under the guise of a simulation, with participant responsibility conferred and then taken away.

On the strongest point of the argument – correct facts – it is necessary to distinguish between the fictitious 'facts' – the Blogsville Company's production costs, the Ruritanian defence treaty, etc – and the non-fictitious facts, the real facts of the outside world which may impinge on the action. In the first case, no 'facts' will have been learned incorrectly; the only incorrect learning is the fictions. As in everyday life people make errors, read documents incorrectly, and so on, and in a simulation they should pay the normal penalties for carelessness, and not have the facilitator protect them from the folly of their ways.

On the question of real 'facts' being given incorrectly, these are either in the documents or they are not. If they are in the documents, the author or publisher is in error or the facts are out of date. The facilitator should have done something about it before the simulation began. If the 'facts' are not in the documents, they are nothing but allegations made by individual participants and should, as in everyday life, go uncorrected if they pass unnoticed. The facilitator can, of course, make a note of the incorrect allegations and point these out in the debriefing, but he should never interrupt a simulation simply to correct facts. Interventions of this sort disrupt the flow, diminish student responsibility and ownership, constrain behaviour for fear of 'getting it wrong', cause resentment, and open the door to an attitude of 'Now we are back in school again'.

The only case in which intervention regarding 'facts' is justified is when the participants get it wrong in a big way, and are under such a serious delusion that the simulation itself is imperilled. In this case, the best thing is for the facilitator to break off the simulation at a convenient point and correct the misunderstanding by whatever method seems the most plausible, depending on the nature of the simulation.

Even when using a simulation to teach English as a second language, the teacher is well advised not to intervene to correct linguistic and grammatical errors. The teacher has to ask the question whether it is to be a simulation or a linguistic exercise, whether the aim is error-free language or successful communication. In this context Kerr (1977) says:

> In the course of a simulation, the teacher may be tempted to intervene when mistakes are made, or even to introduce brief spells of remedial teaching. In general, this is unsatisfactory from several points of view; the student being corrected finds that his train of thought has been interrupted, while the teacher will probably find that the students are not paying full attention to his explanations, but are anxious to proceed with the simulation. Experience has shown that it is better for the teacher to sit in the background with a note-pad, jotting down errors as they occur. It is usually convenient to timetable a remedial teaching lesson (immediately after the simulation ends) in which important mistakes can be discussed and remedial practice takes place. Another possibility is to tape record all or part of the simulation and play back the

recording to the students afterwards, inviting them to identify their own mistakes as they listen.

This advice about recording a simulation can be useful in contexts other than learning English as a foreign language. Many people speak badly or mumble or fail to put forward their ideas in a way that can be understood. Even reading aloud is a dying art, with the person concentrating so hard on looking at the black print that each word comes out but the meaning stays behind. A tape recording helps to illustrate the point. On the other hand, there are dangers that the intrusion of recording apparatus could inhibit the participants. If tape recorders are to be used, they should be used as often as possible so that the participants get used to them and forget about them.

DEBRIEFING

In the follow-up discussion or debriefing, the facilitator returns to the role of teacher or instructor. The transition need not be abrupt, however, since it may be a good idea to allow one (or two) of the participants to take the chair, particularly if the simulation itself involved this sort of function. In this case, the facilitator's contribution would have the same status in procedural terms as that of the students; for example, in giving an account of what the mechanical problems of the simulation were and how the facilitator tackled them.

As a general pattern it is useful to go round the table and have the participants explain their own parts in the simulation – what they saw as the nature of the problems and how they dealt with them. Each participant would contribute to the sum of knowledge, which would be particularly useful if there was a divergence in roles and functions. It also adds to the practice in communication skills to be able to explain what one did and why.

The second stage, after everyone has had their say (without comments or discussion), involves general discussion. The obvious way into this general debate is by looking at the immediate specific questions relating to the outcome – the inquest on the result. But this should not be allowed to degenerate into a rerun of the arguments used within the simulation.

In other words, the debriefing should move fairly rapidly from the particular to the general. The real value in a simulation will be in the transfer of knowledge and experience to other situations in the future. This is likely to involve general principles – how did the groups organize themselves and was the organization effective? What alternatives were there? Did the group or individuals explore the options, analyse the nature of the situation in which they found themselves, and plan accordingly? How effective was the communication? Were the language and behaviour suitable and appropriate? What lessons did the participants learn? Would they act differently when faced with such a situation in the future?

The facilitator may also be keen to get the reactions of the students to the simulation itself – its materials, mechanics and general situation. Here it may be necessary to interpret various remarks. If a student says, 'That was great fun', the comment can mean that the simulation was not much else. If someone says, 'I lost my bit of paper' instead of 'I lost my housing document', this may indicate a lack of realism in the materials. 'I got bored during the last part' could mean that the participant had a part-time or passive role, or that the facilitator had not presented the simulation in a satisfactory manner.

Should the students say, 'We'd like to have another go', it could mean that the teacher should have considered the possibilities of a rerun and reached a decision on whether to have one or not or leave it to a vote. Naturally, if there is a rerun, it is advisable to postpone the debriefing or to curtail it, otherwise too many hints and pieces of advice may be given. But this is a matter for on-the-spot judgement.

In a simulation with a hidden agenda a thorough debriefing is usually essential. This is particularly true in behavioural simulations. These simulations are likely to stir up emotions which can last much longer than the simulation itself. Some participants may feel exposed or humiliated. Gaining insights into one's character can be an abrasive experience. Some participants might feel that they have not gained insights, but have been cheated or manipulated into expressing attitudes, views or emotions which are contrary to their characters or personalities. Little advice can be given to the facilitator in such circumstances, since the problems and likely outcome will already have been anticipated and will probably have been the reason for presenting the simulation in the first place. The facilitator should at least make quite sure that there is ample time in the debriefing to explain why the simulation had a hidden agenda and what it was supposed to reveal.

Debriefings are often missed opportunities. Frequently the debriefing is:

(a) too brief;
(b) too dictatorial;
(c) too routine and unimaginative; and
(d) follows so closely upon the event that mature reflection is excluded.

As suggested earlier in this section, the format of a debriefing can involve the participants, and this can be a subject for negotiation and thus regarded as an imaginative extension of the event itself. For example, it is quite easy to make the debriefing take the form of a public opinion poll. Each ex-participant is given a clipboard on which a question is written. Their job is to get answers to their own question from as many ex-participants as possible, and provide answers to the questions asked by others. This is not done as a committee meeting with one person speaking at a time but by standing up and moving around from person to person.

The question on each clipboard can be decided by the facilitator, or by a committee, or by the pollster. The questions could cover any of the issues already mentioned, either in general terms or related to particular issues:

– How well did the journalists do their job?
– Was the language of the judge suitable for the occasion?
– 'Mistakes are a good thing in simulations.' Do you agree with this statement?
– What advice would you give to the facilitator?
– What was your main problem and how did you deal with it?
– Were your space crew colleagues friendly and helpful?
– What was your opinion of the landlord?
– When some participants asked for help, the facilitator said, 'I'm not in the boardroom (newsroom, etc)'. Should help have been given?

When the poll has been completed then various things could happen. The ex-participants could form themselves into groups and collate the results. There could be a general session in which everyone reads out some or all of the answers on their sheets followed by discussions of those answers that were the most interesting, or educational, or revealing. Alternatively, each person could present their own brief research report, outlining their conclusions as well as giving the evidence.

The above example is a debriefing organized as a research project. It would not be particularly suitable for routine committee simulations where everyone saw and heard everything, but it would fit in with simulations which had hidden agendas or group interactions. Also, a debriefing in this form adds interest and diversity to the communication skills.

If the simulation was a behavioural one with a high level of personal involvement then an immediate debriefing allows people to get things off their chests, and this is important otherwise dissent and bad temper can spill over inside and outside the classroom. However, there is a case for deferring at least the main part of the debriefing until another day. This not only allows time for passions to cool and mature reflection to occur, but it also allows a more structured appraisal. With a structured debriefing there could be written reports or prepared speeches. Different issues could be negotiated or allocated. One person or team could report and comment on what happened in the media group before the broadcast. Other people could look at anxieties, or carry out research into differences and similarities between the event and the real world.

Another virtue of delay is that it can benefit the facilitator. Instead of a snap judgement, a delay gives time for a leisurely recall of what was seen and heard and a mental review of what was significant or interesting. Quite often this review in tranquillity turns up interesting aspects, particularly if there is a recording of the event and the facilitator can listen or look at what went on. Of course, recordings can take a long time to transcribe and usually this is not worth the effort, but there are occasions when a few minutes of transcribed argument or discussion can be highly illuminating. And if copies are run off then this also makes the students feel that the facilitator is really interested in their behaviour. To give just one personal example, a 16-year-old Sudanese girl was the chairperson of a parliamentary committee. She had the job of saying 'Stand up, sit down, shut up.' Listening to the tape revealed that she found 45 different ways of saying this. At first she used the words 'will' and 'would' ('Will/would you please stand up') but later she used 'may' ('You may stand up'). Although 'may' is the politer form, in this case it probably meant 'I have found that you do what I tell you, so I can afford to be polite to you, and my politeness is also a demonstration of my authority'.

Such isolated incidents may seem trivial, but if several of them are mentioned in the debriefing then they can add up to useful insights into behaviour. After all, the whole point of experiential learning is to learn from experience and modify subsequent behaviour, and small points are often more useful, more personal and more meaningful to individuals than broad judgements.

The importance given to the debriefing reflects the value of the simulation experience. To allow a simulation to overrun and then have a five-minute question and answer session is to diminish the educational significance of simulations in the eyes of the participants, and also inadvertently to belittle their own efforts. Truncated debriefings may influence behaviour adversely in the next simulation, leading to less professional attitudes and less personal involvement.

Perhaps the most helpful advice is for the facilitator to consider the options, the timing and the format of the debriefing before running the simulation, preferably in consultation with the participants.

Chapter 6

Assessment

AIMS OF ASSESSMENT

Research and evaluation is an area of controversy in simulation literature, as indeed it is in education generally. The debate is usually on whether the methodology and design of the experiment is appropriate and whether the findings justify the conclusions. But from the point of view of the teacher, there is nothing forbidden, or even forbidding, about assessment in relation to simulations.

Assessment does not imply some grandiose pie-in-the-sky research project to test the hypothesis that 'simulations produce greater gains in critical thinking, decision-making and problem-solving than do other learning methods', or some such similar generalization. Many authors have pointed to the unavoidable difficulties of such attempts. Davison and Gordon (1978) point out that no evaluatory instruments can readily encompass the many different dimensions of behaviour and experience involved, and Twelker (1977) emphasizes the problems caused by the great differences between individual simulations and between the conditions in which they are used. In the jargon of research, there are bound to be a great many uncontrolled variables.

The teacher, therefore, should aim only for what is functional and practical. The idea should simply be to learn something – something about the individual simulation, the participants, and also the teacher's own thoughts and behaviour.

It is a pity that virtually all writers on simulations talk about assessment and evaluation exclusively from the point of view of assessing a simulation. The only criterion seems to be whether the simulation is useful, appropriate, stimulating, etc.

For the teacher, this is a restrictive way of thinking about assessment since it is only half the picture. Just as people can assess simulations, so can simulations be used to assess people. As well as examining simulations, simulations can be examinations. Organizations that have been using simulations the longest – the armed forces and the higher levels of the civil service – use some simulations for the specific purpose of testing.

At staff colleges, on courses at country houses and in the interiors of ministries and large organizations, simulations are used, together with puzzles, problems, case studies, discussions etc, as devices not just for training, but also for assessing the participants.

Once the instructor, tutor, consultant or teacher becomes familiar with a particular puzzle, simulation etc, it can be used to increasing effect for assessment. Practice and experience are needed, as in any other field. There is nothing mysterious about it, nothing really difficult, as every teacher is a professional assessor.

ASSESSING ORAL SKILLS

Teachers who have not been used to running interactive events in their classroom have viewed the prospect of assessing oral skills in such events with some trepidation. It is one thing to assess a formal standardized oral test where each candidate takes it in turn to give a prepared speech, but quite another to assess the subtle and dynamic oral exchanges which occur in simulations, role play and non-taught exercises.

This anxiety is almost entirely due to unfamiliarity with interactive learning. There is nothing especially difficult about assessing oral skills in such contexts. Here are some of the factors that suggest that anxieties are due to an incorrect view of the situation.

1. Oral assessment is based on common sense and experience. Everyone forms impressions about whether the people they meet speak effectively. It is not difficult to tell whether a person is using language that is appropriate to the occasion.
2. Because simulations are untaught events there is ample opportunity for the facilitator to see and hear what goes on. Furthermore, if the debriefing is delayed for a day or two this allows the facilitator to approach the task of observation singlemindedly, without interrupting the observation by mentally working out what instant judgements might be made immediately the event ends.
3. Because the facilitator already knows the materials on which the event is based, and may have run the same simulation before, the talk will not come as a complete surprise. This makes it easier to note what is said, and also what is not said.
4. The facilitator does not enter a debriefing unaccompanied. Self-assessments by the ex-participants are part of the evidence. If recordings or transcripts are available from the event then this also can enhance the assessment.

In assessing oral skills most authorities favour a general impression mark since this allows the event to be judged as a whole. However, there are also plenty of lists of categories which can be borne in mind, consciously or subconsciously. For example:

1. The selection of information/ideas.
2. The order and sequence of presentation.
3. The use of language which is appropriate to the occasion.
4. The clarity – enunciating the words, appropriate pace and volume.
5. Fluency and self-confidence.
6. Effective listening and responding to others.

A search through the publications of the examination boards will reveal pages of categories in which the candidates should 'appreciate the need for...', 'understand the developmental structure of...' and 'be aware that...'. But without actual examples these lists can be more intimidating than enlightening.

They also give the impression of being absolute standards, yet in certain situations there may be an irreconcilable conflict between categories. If one is requesting help from a stranger then a fluent appeal for assistance (item 5) might be counter-productive or inappropriate (item 3). The ability to listen sympathetically when someone is angry or distressed and to mutter an occasional 'Yes' may well be the most appropriate reaction (item 3), whereas an attempt to interrupt and give an orderly presentation of information/ideas (item 2) could be interpreted as an unfriendly gesture designed to show superiority.

Lists of categories give the impression that they are designed to assess a set speech, not an interactive event. So when assessing the oral skills in simulations a useful starting point could be the four questions mentioned in the chapter on Design: What is the problem? Who are the participants? What do they have to do? What do they do it with? Assessment must depend on the assessor knowing each individual situation, and it really cannot be done by merely looking at the words and consulting a list of categories. Basing the assessment on what actually happens rather than on predetermined categories opens the door to unexpected findings.

ASSESSING BEHAVIOUR

Some organizations use simulations and role-play exercises as tests not only of language and communications but also of behaviour. Contact between a member of an organization and someone outside involves behaviour, and the organization is usually very concerned to see that the behaviour is appropriate and effective. In certain jobs and professions, both appointments and promotions depend a great deal on behaviour.

Sometimes the assessment is recorded formally. For example, if the simulation involves an interview of some sort (appointments board, personal interview, media interview) there may be a standard form for the instructor, tutor, consultant, etc to record the result such as:

Criterion	Standard achieved			Remarks
	Above average	Average	Below average	
Posture and deportment				
Clarity of expression				
Confidence				
etc				

But whether the assessment is formal or informal, the main question to be asked is whether the behaviour is appropriate to the circumstances. This question can be asked about any participant in any simulation. Depending on the participant's function and the specific job and circumstances, the question can be divided up into various parts. For example:

- ability to make a point
- ability to stick to the point
- ability to search for options
- ability to work out possible consequences
- degree of courteousness, sympathy, understanding, honesty, diplomacy, etc.

These ideas can form the basis of a teacher's assessment of the behaviour of participants during a simulation.

IN-DEPTH INTERVIEWS

Assessment can be retrospective. As well as observing what happens during a simulation, the teacher can use in-depth interviews after the simulation to assess both the participants and the simulation itself.

This can be regarded as a supplement to the debriefing. It can cover similar ground, but whereas the debriefing is often generalized, the interview can get down to the particular and the individual. Since debriefing sessions often tend to be on the skimpy side, the interview can be a highly valuable tool of assessment and learning. Its value lies in revealing what otherwise might remain unknown or obscure.

In-depth interviewing is rather like beachcombing. All sorts of interesting and curious things come to light, some of them most unexpected. It can reveal insights into attitudes, events and motives which range much wider than the preceding simulation event.

The interviewer will normally be the facilitator, but other options could also be considered – a colleague, an observer, an ex-participant, a student from another class, a visitor. Here are a few extracts of comments from children in multiracial classes during interviews with the author.

A 16-year-old Moroccan boy in secondary school after a simulation involving Private Members' bills:

> We've done this and the teacher's out of it, right? And everyone is responsible for their own working. Because, normally, I'm quite good at English, and yet this still increases your knowledge about the world. Like some of the words that we put down here I would never use. I'd never use them, I'd never think of using them. I mean, instead of saying 'offence' I'd say 'a crime'. We would not say 'male' or 'female', we'd say 'boy' or 'girl'. And 'sexual pleasure', we would not even say 'sexual', we'd say 'sex' and that's it. I mean, it's the way we speak. Actually doing this sort of thing we actually learned sort of how law English is.

A 16-year-old Italian girl in secondary school after the simulation TELEVISION CORRESPONDENT (Jones 1987):

> Doing the usual lesson is so easy for us because all we have to do is to write it out, and the teacher tells me that this is good, good, good, and I know what to put in it already and it is easy for me to put it on paper and just finish it up. But when I come to this then I quite like it. I am for once understanding what I am doing. I am using difficult words but I understand them. But in a normal lesson, you are just guessing.

A 16-year-old girl, also after participating in TELEVISION COR-RESPONDENT:

It teaches you more ... I mean ... if the teacher says to do something, OK you understand me, and you kind of argue, the teacher is bound to tell you the answer because there are so many people in the class, and they just give you the answer and not explain what is going on as they have to go to the next person who needs help. But once you are cooperating all together and sitting down and doing it on your own ... and I find it really interesting, and it's really good, and it's really helpful.

Some of the points are shrewd. The Italian girl makes a contrast between what is easy and what is understood – most people would assume that these always go together. All the speakers showed natural verbal ability, and the use of repetition in making their points is impressive.

QUESTIONNAIRES

Questionnaires are probably the most common tool for:

(a) assessing the participants' behaviour/skills/learning;
(b) evaluating and comparing simulations as events.

Usually questionnaires are tailormade by the teacher (or participants, research worker, author) to fit particular events. They can be used for small groups or for much larger experiments. They can be used after the simulation, or both before and after.

There are problems. Bloomer (1974) remarks: 'Questionnaires are prone to the danger that the teacher discovers not what has been learnt, nor even what the pupils thought they had learnt, but only what the teacher would like them to have learnt.' This touches on one of the main problems – what questions to ask? If the teacher limited the questions to the main objectives for introducing the simulation in the first place, the answers will similarly be limited and the questionnaire will not reveal whether any non-specified objectives were achieved.

It is useful, therefore, for the questionnaire to cover skills as well as facts, emotions as well as subjects, and behaviour as well as learning. Fishing with open-ended questions is revealing: 'One important thing that I found in taking part in the simulation was...' However, it is preferable to put the open-ended questions first in the questionnaire. If they are added at the end of a list of factual questions, the participants may simply trot out another fact. Here are some sample questions:

The thing that surprised me was...
Comment about anything that mattered to you as a person...
How did your talking help your thinking?
How did you behave?
Compared with your objectives, did you find what you did satisfactory?
Was the decision-making in your team democratic?
Did you learn anything about being diplomatic?
Would you have liked more time for any of the parts in the simulation?
Did you think it gave you useful practice in...?
How could you have done better?
Did you consider ethics or only material values?
Would you have introduced the simulation any differently?

If the questionnaire is to be used for statistical purposes, some questions must have quantifiable answers. They can be

Yes ☐   No ☐

or

Yes				No

or

Very enjoyable						Very miserable

Statistics derived from such questionnaires can be not only misleading, but sometimes the exact opposite of what they are assumed to indicate. An illustration of this is the figure of 3.6 per cent of participants who listed themselves as being 'totally uninterested' after a large-scale current affairs simulation that lasted for two days at a polytechnic. The implication was that the 3.6 per cent were uninterested in current affairs or the simulation or both. It is the sort of statistic that causes authors to say, 'Yes, we know that there is usually a small percentage of participants who don't like simulations, and here's another example of this'.

Yet on questioning the authors of the research report, it turned out that the participants who had graded themselves as 'totally uninterested' were all members of the team representing the Advisory, Conciliation and Arbitration Service. No other team called them in. They were unemployed. They had sat around for two days doing nothing except watch the other participants enjoy themselves. They were not protesting against participation in the simulation: they were protesting against non-participation.

Questionnaires should not be used in isolation from other assessments and should be supported by an adequate description of what actually happened in the simulation in question.

Two other points can be made. First, it is better to have a questionnaire covering two or more simulations than just one. With one simulation the questions tend to float about in the air. What does 'enjoyable' mean? Enjoyable compared with what? With another simulation, with a lesson in mathematics, with a favourite television programme?

Words like 'useful', 'interesting', 'valuable' derive their meaning from comparisons, and if comparisons are not specified, the whole operation takes on a random flavour with many participants deciding to play cautiously and place the tick in the middle of the range of values.

Secondly, a questionnaire requires to be interpreted in the light of the previous experience of the participants. If they have never taken part in a simulation before their replies to questions may include an extra element of uncertainty, misunderstanding and unfamiliarity because the first simulation is usually the most difficult one.

Summary

The following ten points sum up some of the key issues in this book.

1. For the purposes of this book, the differences between simulations, games, exercises, and role play are best determined by the thoughts and behaviour of the participants, rather than by the label on the box or the terminology of the facilitator.

2. A simulation is characterized by functional roles (journalist, prime minister, and so on) plus sufficient information on an issue or problem to allow the participants to function as 'professionals'.

3. Whereas a simulation can, and often does, involve real-world ethics, a game has its own magic kingdom of rules where the main duty is to try to win and, apart from fair play, real-world ethics have no place.

4. It is not an essential characteristic of a simulation to imitate real life. Simulations can involve fantasy, or fiction, or stand real life on its head. However, it is the environment of a simulation that is simulated, the participants do not simulate, they keep their own personalities and do the best they can in the situation in which they find themselves.

5. For any kind of teaching or training that involves behaviour, simulations are a most powerful tool. Good simulations are highly memorable and can have a profound effect on personal development. Learning can occur not only during the

event and in the debriefing but days or weeks later. Areas where simulations are often part-and-parcel of education and training include the armed forces, businesses, areas dealing with economic, social and cultural issues and language teaching. A particularly fruitful area is that of inter-cultural simulations and simulations involving ethical issues, not only the 'outside ethics' of the real world, but the 'inside ethics' involving the thoughts, emotions, attitudes, and behaviour of participants within the events.

6. During the action, the facilitator should adopt a hands-off approach and allow participants full authority within their roles, including the power to make mistakes, otherwise the simulation may turn into a guided exercise.

7. For participants new to simulations, and for participants who may be expecting games, exercises, or role play, it is strongly advised that the briefing should explain the 'professional' nature of the behaviour required – no play acting, no mimicry, and no gaming behaviour – and that real-life consequences should be considered. For example, to obtain a business contract by deception may secure an immediate 'gain', but could involve long-term damage to the company's reputation, as well as being unethical behaviour.

8. An ambivalent is an event in which different and incompatible methodologies are operating simultaneously. In most cases, ambivalents include players trying to 'win', while the other participants are in the simulation mode, accepting real-world ethics. Simulations can also be contaminated if one or more role cards invite the participants to play act, rather than behave professionally. Ambivalents are dangerous and should be avoided in almost all cases. Not only can they cause hurt and distress but the cause, the methodological muddle, is likely to go undetected. Clashes of methodology are often interpreted as being clashes of personalities. A particular type of hurtful ambivalent is when some participants are encouraged to behave like players in a game and are subsequently criticized for trying to 'win' rather than working for the community. There are some interesting but rare cases of 'necessary ambivalents', where the events would not work properly unless some partici-

pants behaved like gamesters, while others adopted real-world ethics.

9. All simulations require adequate debriefing. Particularly careful debriefing is required for any event which could cause emotional and psychological damage or which involves author/facilitator deceit.

10. Simulations can be used not only for teaching and training, but also for assessment. Indeed, their first organized use, in the Prussian army, was for the purpose of a better selection of officers. Simulations can be used to assess communication skills, language skills, oral skills, decision-making, diplomacy, organizational skills and personal development. Not only are simulations effective learning devices, they are usually highly stimulating and motivational.

Appendix

DETECTIVE STORY

DETECTIVE STORY is referred to in the text, page 78. It is taken from my book *Icebreakers: A Sourcebook of Games, Exercises and Simulations*. This simulation is unusual because of the roles – the participants are ideas in the mind of a writer of detective stories who has writer's block. However, the format is not unusual and an examination of the mechanics of the event will reveal one way in which a simulation took shape. The documents are:

Facilitator's notes
Participants' notes
Eight character cards (Aunt, Butler, Lady Eve, Lord Adam, Maid, Detective, Smith, and Son)
Ideas sheet to record information and propose a story line.

This simulation, also an icebreaker, is complete in itself and can be photocopied and used within the institution purchasing this book.

DETECTIVE STORY   Facilitator's notes

DETECTIVE STORY is a simulation in which the participants are ideas for characters in an unwritten detective story in the mind of a famous author who has a mental block. The block prevents the ideas from joining together as a group. Participants meet in pairs to try to get the story moving again.

Numbers
The minimum is about eight although it might work with fewer by omitting a card, or giving two cards to one participant. There is no maximum.

Materials
One copy for each participant of **Ideas Sheet** (cloudy shapes). One sheet of **Character Cards** for every eight participants. Keep each set together, as with numbers larger than eight there is a danger of having too many of one card and too few (or none) of another. Note that if two people meet and have an identical card they merge into the same idea and must stick together.

Procedure
Hand out the Participants' Notes to all the participants and retrieve the document before the action begins. Hand out the Ideas Sheet. The Character Cards can be placed face down and the participants can pick their own. Arrange the room like a brain (a classroom with rows of desks perhaps) with lots of pathways intersecting and diverging.

Debriefing
Make arrangements for participants to announce their initiatives. The discussion could cover the question of how the participants cooperated and sent messages to each other. Did they use any procedure for collecting information and coordinating ideas?

DETECTIVE STORY   Participants' notes

DETECTIVE STORY is a simulation in which the participants are ideas for characters in an unwritten detective story in the mind of a famous author who has a mental block. The block prevents the ideas from joining together as a group. Participants meet in pairs to try to get the story moving again.

You will receive, at random, a **Character Card**, which gives you the name of the character together with something they said. There is no information about who your character was speaking to, or the circumstances, or whether the statement was true or false. Show the card to each participant you meet as you circulate around the brain. You will also receive an **Ideas Sheet**.

At the start meet only in pairs and make each meeting extremely brief. The writer's block does not permit threes or larger groups except if you come across someone with the same Character Card as your own – and you then become the same idea, and stick together like linked neurons.

Later, when you have met at least half of the other ideas, you can start to form into pairs if you find you are thinking on similar lines. The pairs can grow into trios and larger groups. Use the Ideas Sheet to record information, propose a story line, and make amendments. It shows your development as an idea, and like all ideas you can grow, marry and create. The Ideas Sheet is not confidential – reveal it to the other ideas you meet.

You are not looking for a story that is there. Your author did not think of a story and then forget it. Your author created a few characters and snippets of dialogue for a detective story but had a mental block before deciding who did what and which were the red herrings. Thus, you are an unemployed idea. You want work and you want to develop. The more agreement there is on a story line the more chance there is of nudging your author back into creativity. In this way you can achieve a purposeful and memorable life.

DETECTIVE STORY

AUNT

And I shall have no hesitation in striking you out of my will.

BUTLER

I shall endeavour not to mention it.

LADY EVE

My husband, as you must be fully aware, is a gambler.

LORD ADAM

I would have you know that I am faithful to my wife.

Character Cards

MAID

One day this could be mine.

DETECTIVE

What made you think it was a forgery?

SMITH

We want to buy the estate and turn it
into a theme park.

SON

I am not on drugs.

DETECTIVE STORY

Ideas Sheet

References

Abt, C C (1968) Games for learning. In Boocock, S S and Schild, E O (eds) *Simulation Games in Learning* Sage, Thousand Oaks, California

Bloomer, J (1974) Outsider; pitfalls and payoffs of simulation gaming *SAGSET Journal* **4**, 3

Coleman, B (1977) Videorecording and STARPOWER. *SAGSET Journal* **3**, 1. Also published in Megarry, J (ed) (1977) *Aspects of Simulation and Gaming* Kogan Page, London

Davison, A and Gordon, P (1978) *Games and Simulations in Action* Woburn Press, London

Druckman, D (1994) Tools for discovery: Experimenting with simulations *Simulation & Gaming*, **25**, 4

Duke, R D (1979) Nine steps to game design. In *How to Build a Simulation/Game*, the proceedings of the 10th ISAGA conference, Leeuwarden, the Netherlands, vol. 1, 98–112. Also reprinted in Greenblat, C S and Duke, R D (1981) *Principles and Practices of Gaming-Simulation* Sage, California and London

Elgood, C (1976) *Handbook of Management Games* Gower Press, Farnborough

Gredler, M (1992) *Designing and Evaluating Games and Simulations: A Process Approach* Kogan Page, London

Greenblat, C S (1986) *Capjefos: A Simulation of Village Development*. Available from Dept of Sociology, Rutgers University, New Brunswick, New Jersey

Jones, K (1985) *Designing Your Own Simulations* Methuen, London

Jones, K (1987) *Six Simulations* (SPACE CRASH, MASS MEETING, THE RAG TRADE, BANK FRAUD, TELEVISION CORRESPONDENT, THE LINGUAN PRIZE FOR LITERATURE) Simon & Schuster, London

Jones, K (1988) *Interactive Learning Events: A Guide for Facilitators* Kogan Page, London and Nichols Publishing, New York

Jones, K (1989) *A Sourcebook of Management Simulations* Kogan Page, London and Nichols Publishing, New York

Jones, K (1991) *Icebreakers: A Sourcebook of Games, Exercises and Simulations* Kogan Page, London and Pfeiffer, San Diego

Jones, K (1993) *Imaginative Events: A Sourcebook of innovative simulations, exercises, puzzles and games* (two volumes; HUMAN ZOO is in vol. 1 McGraw-Hill, Maidenhead. Also published by McGraw-Hill, New York under the title *Imaginative Events for Training: A Trainer's Sourcebook of Games, Simulations and Role-Play Exercises* (one volume)

Kerr, J Y K (1977) Games and simulations in English-language teaching. In *Games, Simulations and Role-playing* British Council, London

Kirts, C A, Tumeo, M A, and Sinz, J M (1991) The COMMONS GAME: Its instructional value when used in a national resources management context. *Simulation & Gaming*, **22**, 1

Klabbers, J and Hearn, J (1988) Policy formation through simulation and communication. In Crookall, D and Saunders, D (eds) *Communication and Simulation: From Two Fields to One Theme* Multilingual Matters, Clevedon, Avon and Philadelphia, PA

Liebrand, W B G (1983) A classification of social dilemma games. *Simulation & Games*, **14**, 2

Moses, J L (1977) The assessment center method. In Moses, J L and Byham, W C (eds) *Applying the Assessment Center Method* Pergamon Press, Oxford

OSS (1948) *Assessment of Men, Selection of Personnel for the Office of Strategic Services* Rinehart, New York

Petranek, C (1994) A maturation in experiential learning: Principles of simulation and gaming. *Simulation & Gaming*, **25**, 4

Powers, R B and Boyle, W (1983) Generalization from a commons-dilemma game. *Simulation & Games*, **14**, 3

Powers, R B, Duus, R E, and Norton, R S (1983) The COMMONS GAME. Unpublished research manuscript. Utah State University, Logan

Ravensdale (1978) The dangers of competition. *SAGSET Journal*, **8**, 3

Shirts, R G (1973) BAFA BAFA Simulation Training Systems, Del Mar, California

Shirts, R G (1969) STARPOWER Simulation Training Systems, Del Mar, California

Stewart, L P (1992) Ethical issues in postexperimental and post-experiential debriefing. *Simulation & Gaming*, **23**, 2

Tesch, F E (1977) Debriefing research participants: Though this be method there is madness in it. *Journal of Personality and Social Psychology*, **35**, 217–224

Twelker, P A (1977) Some reflections on the innovation of simulation and gaming. In Megarry, J (ed) *Aspects of Simulation and Gaming* Kogan Page, London

Vernon, R F (1978) TALKING ROCKS Simulation Training Systems, Del Mar, California

Walster, E, Berscheid, E, Abrahams, D, and Aronson, V (1967) Effectiveness of debriefing following deception experiments. *Journal of Personality and Social Psychology*, **6**, 371–380

Zuckerman, D W and Horn, R E (1973) (eds) *The Guide to Simulations/Games for Education and Training* Information Resources Inc, Lexington

CPSIA information can be obtained
at www.ICGtesting.com
Printed in the USA
LVOW07s1400061017
551459LV00018B/290/P